WORKSHOP ON
UNIVERSAL RESPONSIBILITY

INDIA INTERNATIONAL CENTRE
November 16th 1991

INTRODUCTION

RAJIV MEHROTRA: This workshop is the first event organised by the Foundation for Universal Responsibility. The corpus fund for the Foundation comes from the Nobel Peace Prize money. We are still completing our registration formalities with the Government of India to enable us to be fully functional. We hope to be an organisation based in India but reaching out around the world. We have been overwhelmed by the support we have received from so many quarters.

The Foundation seeks to cultivate and catalyse a sense of Universal Responsibility, a response to the world's needs as a kind of reflex, a natural function of the silent mind, rather than as an end-product of a series of complicated moral or logical decisions. Of course, in the long run our decisions and actions must stand up to the scrutiny of sophisticated moral and logical imperatives. However, most intimately and frequently our responses are untutored impulses.

Universal Responsibility is the perfect embodiment of compassion. Compassion is the everyday face of wisdom. It dissolves in the otherness of the other; it recognises that we can eliminate suffering and find happiness ourselves when we recognise that every problem on our earth, now even in the skies above us, is our own personal responsibility. This realisation will occur when division and strife between ideologies, religions, peoples and nations cease, when we recognise our interdependence. When we recognise and experience our interconnectedness, powerlessness dissolves in the face of that sense of oneness.

The fact is that we do have power, the power and energy that come from doing things for other people, from standing up for them, from manifesting altruism bred from a shared sense of community. The Foundation seeks to empower people, to catalyse, to build bridges of understanding and co-operation amongst themselves and between organisations, cultures and ideologies.

While drawing its inspiration from the Tibetan Buddhist tradition of combining spirituality with practicality in a pragmatic way, the Foundation does not seek to promote any one political ideology, religion, philosophy, individual or cause. By its very nature Universal Responsibility is a bringing together, a reaching out to all. Ours must be a path that is both walked and talked. The burning energy of Universal Responsibility must be kindled and governed by an understanding of the suffering that individuals experience, of social problems and social change.

Today, at this workshop, the Foundation hopes to learn from the experience and insights of some of the best Indian scholars and activists. It hopes in the process to provide a context for you to interact with each other, to encourage a sharing, an articulation of intuitions and a reaching out to others, a commitment both to listen and to talk, to create an impetus for action. I welcome all of you here as an affirmation of that commitment.

I ask you to bear with us for the hiccups along the way, for our lack of experience in putting something like this workshop together; and I seek your indulgence for having intervened for so long between the wisdom of a true Master and its sharing with all of us. I have the faith that together, today, we will take that one small step firmly towards a commitment to Universal Responsibility.

H.H. THE DALAI LAMA: Friends, today we have an opportunity to discuss Universal Responsibility. I would like to thank all those who have made this possible. I understand that in organising this meeting, many people—there are quite a number of new faces, but many familiar faces also, and a familiar subject—have displayed a great deal of interest and have volunteered to help. I feel that this itself is a manifestation of Universal Responsibility.

I am very happy to have an opportunity to discuss, and to listen to other views on Universal Responsibility. This is the first opportunity I have had to discuss these matters in India, where much has been written and spoken about infinite compassion, infinite altruism and *ahimsa* over thousands of years. The idea of Universal Responsibility itself developed out of ancient Indian thought. These are very important ideas which I have learnt from this country; I am very, very happy to be here in this sacred land of Arya Bhumi.

4

Everybody here knows about *ahimsa* or non-violence. Non-violence does not mean the absence of violence. It is something more positive and more meaningful. I think the fuller expression of non-violence is compassion. Some people have the impression that compassion is something akin to pity. I think that is not the correct understanding. Genuine compassion is a closeness of feeling with, and at the same time a sense of responsibility for, the other person's welfare. True compassion develops when we accept the other as a being just like us, a being who wants happiness and does not want suffering.

True compassion comes when we develop a genuine concern about someone else's experience of difficulty or pain with an allied sense of responsibility. Once we develop that kind of compassion, we see that it covers all human beings, including our so-called enemies, those people who disturb our mind or hurt us. Irrespective of what they do to us or the effect they have on us, we recognise that all beings have an equal right to be happy. We will then have no problem in developing compassion towards such people. Usually, our compassion or love is biased. It is a feeling we can extend only towards our friends and not towards neutral people, especially not towards those we see as our enemies. That is not genuine compassion. Naturally, once there is the kind of compassion that is truly universal there is a feeling of responsibility that goes with it. The basic meaning of Universal Responsibility is to want to do something for others without a selfish motive, out of a feeling of compassion. That is what I think. The cultivation of compassion is an important part of my daily practice as a Buddhist practitioner. As a Dalai Lama, I have become a refugee and face enormous problems. I often get the feeling that my daily practice of compassion is just sitting in a corner of a room, meditating on compassion. Of course, it is very good, it is very nice and comfortable, but sometimes the idea of Bodhichitta or Bodhisattvahood seems a little vague and remote. Bodhi has a special meaning for Buddhists, but satva is the essence. The meaning of the Tibetan word here is something akin to courageous determination—to think about others and do something for them, extending the sense of our responsibility.

It is very important to implement this, to try to help at least one other being on this planet. It is easier to meditate on this than to find the determination to do something for humanity on this planet. This is my feeling. Sometimes we merely meditate on compassion as if it were something inactive. If there is an opportunity to do something, that should form the basis of meditation. It needs to be the motivation for the meditator to express his or her sense of Universal Responsibility.

I consider the purpose of our lives to be the cultivation of happiness and joy—whether we are rich or poor, educated or uneducated, and irrespective of nationality, colour, social status and ideology. In order to achieve that, material development is important. But it is equally important to develop the inner qualities of spiritual development. Unless our mental attitude is stable and calm, the effectiveness of external actions is limited. Therefore, inner development is important in order to achieve a happy life and a happy future.

One of the most effective destroyers of our mental calm is hatred. This is very clear. The antidote is compassion. So the practice of compassion is not something sacred nor is it a religious or holy practice. It is a human quality. Basically human nature is loving. I do not agree with people who believe that human nature is aggressive. Of course aggressiveness, anger and hatred are a part of human nature. However, I do not think these are dominant forces in the human personality. The dominant quality of human nature is compassion. From the day of our birth to the day of our death, the most important factor in our lives is human affection. We could not survive without it.

If we let hatred and anger run our lives, our physical body also deteriorates; whereas our body gets healthier and healthier if we remain calm and compassionate and are open-minded. Clearly, even the physical body benefits from positive thinking, while a negative mental attitude harms our physical health.

The more compassionate the society and the more compassionate the family, the happier the members of that community and family will be. Every action carried out with that motivation and in that kind of atmosphere is fruitful and successful. If instead there is hatred, anger or jealousy, we may succeed for a short time and our actions may appear more effective but we will not get satisfactory results in the long run. World history itself clearly demonstrates this.

I believe fear is also one of the major obstacles to both inner and outer development. When we do not feel compassion, we have no chance to develop faith. Becoming more compassionate automatically leads to an opening up to our inner problems. As a result, we can communicate with each other with greater honesty and openness and this is one of the most effective ways to reduce fear. On the other hand, if we have less affection and compassion, we automatically look at others as if they also have that kind of temperament. As a result, we close our inner doors. But we have to live in society, so it goes against human nature if we create hostility, through our own negative mental attitudes, between ourselves and the community or group or those individuals on whom we have to depend.

Different religions have a special role to play in the awakening of compassion. Although philosophically there are many differences between them, all of them realise the importance of compassion and have the potential to increase and enhance compassion and harmony. It is on the basis of their common thinking that they can all understand each other and work together.

At the same time, the qualities of compassion and forgiveness are human qualities that form the basis of human survival. They have nothing to do with religion. As a Buddhist, I think religion evolves on the basis of human nature. Religion actually strengthens and increases its positive aspects. But it is compassion rather than religion which is important to us. The population of this planet is about five billion, of which perhaps only about one billion follow a formal religion. The remaining four billion are not religious believers. So if we only talk about religion, then these four billion, this majority group, may not take an interest. But on the other hand, these people, as human brothers and sisters, can be inspired by the need for compassion. Religion involves compassion, but compassion does not necessarily involve religion.

In our present world there are many problems, such as that of the environment. Essentially these are beyond national boundaries. In ancient times each village was more or less independent; there was no need for others' co-operation, because they did everything themselves and they survived. But now the situation has completely changed. National political boundaries seem important, while actually they are not. Something that happens in one area has an impact or implications beyond the boundaries of that area or country.

So we need a broader outlook these days, and the need for a sense of Universal Responsibility is connected with this. The problems that humanity is facing today demand a positive mental attitude and a sense of compassion for others. Not all the problems can be solved easily but at least they can be reduced. This is what I feel.

I would like to add that the idea of compassion originally came from the idea of *ahimsa*. In order to understand *ahimsa* fully and act on the basis of it, some kind of inner disarmament is very important. It is equally important to have external disarmament. A great deal of thought and discussion has been given to disarmament already. I remember when the Chinese attacked India in 1962, I met the President, Dr. Rajendra Prasad. He had already retired to Patna. He said India should unilaterally disarm. At the same time Pandit Nehru as the Prime Minister in Delhi said such a step was impossible, India must get armaments. At that time both positions seemed right. In the short term Pandit Nehru's statement was very correct. But in the long term Rajendra Prasad's statement was right. Thirty years later, East-West tensions seem to have dissolved. The rigid Communist system was a defacto military dictatorship. Except for China, North Korea and Vietnam and perhaps Cuba, the remaining regimes have all gone. The time now has come to think seriously about *ahimsa* and its implementation. We can discuss compassion but there can never be a complete form of *ahimsa* as long as there are weapons. Obviously all it takes is one human being, who may otherwise be very compassionate, to lose his or her temper and resort to the use of these weapons. If there are weapons, there is danger.

Complete disarmament is not impossible. There is at least one demilitarised nation on this planet already—Costa Rica. Over 40 years ago, in 1948, Costa Rica disarmed during a very critical period in a very critical area and it survived. Now, in the changed global situation, there is an even greater need for this kind of responsibility. Along with inner disarmament, therefore, external disarmament is equally important. Several years ago I wrote a booklet called *A Human Approach To World Peace*. Then last year I wrote two booklets, one about Compassion and the other about Disarmament, and in them I wrote about precisely these questions.

8

As a Buddhist and as a Tibetan I feel I am a student of the culture of this great country. Once I sent a congratulatory message letter to Mr. Morarji Desai when he became Prime Minister. He wrote a very beautiful sentence in his reply: "One Bodhi tree has two branches, which are India and Tibet." Culturally and spiritually speaking, we are one people. Emotionally, too, I feel very close to this country, which we call Arya Bhumi. In practical terms this country is the greatest democracy. In spite of a lot of difficulties, it is the world's largest democratic country. In ancient times this country produced many great thinkers, which means that many people took initiatives in philosophy and in spiritual thinking.

In modern India it has become rarer for people to come out with new and original initiatives and ideas because of all the problems. Yet this is a very, very important country with an important role to play. I think it is necessary for you to realise your special responsibility. As this 20th century ends and we enter the 21st century I hope, I wish and I pray that this nation and its people will set an example and contribute by acting on the basis of *ahimsa* and compassion.

Universal Responsibility: The Heritage
Chairperson: Dr. Kapila Vatsyayan

KAPILA VATSYAYAN: His Holiness has articulated in words as much as can be said. He has also made his point by virtue of his very presence which embodies the human heritage itself. Before I call upon the distinguished participants to make their observations in this section, I would just like to say that a section is a segment of the whole. And therefore, both aspects, the universal and responsibility, make up the whole.

To talk of heritage in physical terms would be not only incomplete but also misleading, because the inner landscape of mankind really forms heritage. In that inner landscape is, first and foremost, the outer landscape by which I mean the environment. Man has polluted this by polluting his inner self. That is where the inner and the outer are interconnected. As one looks from heritage to cultures or religions, the point that I would like to stress is the urgency as all cultures have stressed it—that of ecological balance, whether as a religious or cultural world-view. First and foremost is man's awareness of his dependence on the environment and of his being part and parcel of it. Therefore, whatever emerges as the physical expression of that heritage in stone or in paint, in words or in music, in dance or in any other form, arises out of and expresses the ecological balance.

His Holiness has already mentioned the other points which lead us to the topics of chaos, violence, order, *ahimsa*: problems which all texts, religious or otherwise, have dealt with; problems which really emerge from inner fear and desire and outer aggression.

RAFIQ ZAKARIA: I am to present the Islamic view on the question of compassion, *ahimsa*, and Universal Responsibility. I feel that there is more reason today than ever before to understand what Islam stands for in the context of what His Holiness has said.

For the last 1,500 years there has been so much distortion, misrepresentation and even allegations against Islam and its Prophet that the real picture has been completely blurred. So now that we have gathered together to deliberate on Universal Responsibility in the world today, I shall try in my own humble way to remove some of the cobwebs in the minds of non-Muslims about Islam.

A certain historical perspective of the spread of Islam is very necessary for this purpose; Islam spread soon after the passing away of the Prophet, and during his lifetime its expansion was confined to Arabia only. I do not want to go into the question of whether it spread through the sword, because the falsity of this argument has been thoroughly exposed. There is no place for aggression in Islam. The Quran specifically prohibits it. But because it was attacked by its enemies right from its inception, it had to defend itself. And because the poor and down-trodden took to it, their oppressors resisted its spread. The undeniable fact is that it spread at the cost of Christianity in Christian-dominated countries; but it spread because of its teachings. As H.G. Wells, who is not particularly sympathetic to Mohammed or Islam, has pointed out: "Islam prevailed because it was the best social and political order the times could offer. It prevailed because everywhere it found politically apathetic people, robbed, oppressed, bullied, uneducated and unorganised, and it found selfish and unsound governments out of touch with people. It was the broadest, freshest and cleanest political idea that had yet come into an actual active form in the world and it offered better terms than any other to the masses of mankind."

Be that as it may, because of this spread of Islam into the Christian dominions, from the Byzantine Empire to the Holy Roman Empire and into North Africa as well as to other places including Iran, there was a systematic effort on the part of the Christian monks, and even of Christian poets, writers and others, to present Islam as something false, the Prophet as an impostor and the Quran as the concoction of an epileptic mind. Even some of the best minds in the West, including Dante and Voltaire, succumbed to the temptation to perpetuate such misrepresentations with regard to the basic message of Islam.

As this calumny continued, age after age, some impartial observers like Carlyle and Gibbon criticised it in writing. They showed that Islam could not be dismissed as false because its appeal was solid, substantial and highly universal. Yet somehow or the other, through all these centuries the world has been fed on the untruth that Islam is a false religion and in particular that it preaches no compassion, is opposed to human brotherhood and divides the world into Darul-Harab and Darul-Aman, the zone of war and the zone of peace. All these accusations and aberrations have spread through the non-Muslim world. India, too, is not free of their impact, which was systematically created during the days of British colonialism.

I want to stress that Islam emphasises compassion as much His Holiness has highlighted it. The Quran consists of 114 Suras, or chapters, and each of them begins with "Bismillahir Rehmanir Rahim"—"In the name of God the most merciful, the most compassionate." So compassion is stressed again and again. Everywhere in the Quran, and in the life of the Prophet, too, the consistent teaching is that mankind is one, that different religions stress belief in the unity of God. Furthermore, it says that if God had wanted, He would have made all people of one faith but He gave everyone in every land the opportunity to listen to His message and follow the true path as shown by His chosen messengers. There are only two fundamentals which the Quran insists upon: belief in the unity of God, and to do righteous deeds. That is the foundation of the true path to which all were invited by God through His messengers.

Mohammed was clearly told in the Quran that there should be no coercion in religion. How is it, then, that there has been so much confrontation, conflict and even bloodshed in the name of Islam? This has happened because the moment religion gets into the hands of the rulers it becomes a convenient tool to be used for their aggrandisement. In today's world, religious conflict flares up because we emphasise hatred more than love, revenge more than compassion, war more than peace. There is an unseemly competition for superiority and over- lordship. More than in any other religion, I am sorry to say, this is what has been done to Islam by many of its proponents; its basic tenets were violated by most of the Muslim rulers, who used its cover to hide their wrongs. That is why Allama Iqbal, the great poet-philosopher of modern Islam, has said that nothing has harmed Islam more than historical Islam.

We often use the word 'tolerance' when we speak about Universal Responsibility towards man and his welfare. Gandhiji did not like the word tolerance, because he thought it implied a sense of superiority. We tolerate something that we believe is not quite right or correct; it means we are right and the other wrong but we tolerate the one who is in the wrong. But today, Your Holiness, you have emphasised more a spirit of mutual respect, of accommodation of each other's values without denigrating their beliefs. The Quran also says: you have your way, I have mine. True religion can be the best moral force. But we have seen in recent times what has happened to those people who discarded it. After almost 75 years of indoctrination by Communist ideology, the Soviet Union collapsed. There was once again an upsurge in religious practice, replacing the atheistic movements which had preached the denial of spirituality and an unbridled attachment to materialism. History has shown than man cannot live by bread alone.

CHATURVEDI BADRINATH: Let us again ask the question that His Holiness has asked. What is responsibility? This is not a formal academic inquiry, seeking definitions, but it is an important question. There is considerable confusion about it, both in the history of religion and in the history of the secularist political ideologies of the West.

Is the idea of responsibility a commandment of God? Is it a moral 'ought' of some ethical theory? Is it extracted from a particular view of human history? Is it simply a case of answerability to the given laws of society, nothing more than legal accountability to the State? Do these constitute responsibility? Or is the idea of responsibility for others, Universal Responsibility, a product of good-natured but lazy minds, given to dreaming Utopian dreams? Well, if it is the last, then it can be only that, a Utopian dream. It can result in nothing more substantial than finely crafted sentences, beautiful but empty.

Two conclusions can be clearly drawn, I think, from the history of the Semitic faiths, Christianity and Islam. These two conclusions apply also to the secularist ideologies which, at least in theory, break away from any religious presuppositions. In these faiths and ideologies, there is a distinction between being 'answerable to' and 'responsible for'. One is a legalistic idea, the other a profoundly ethical idea which arises in Christianity in the

14

form of Jesus. He breaks away from the Judaic idea of answerability to God, answerability to the law; and he propounds love instead. He substitutes love for laws. That became perfectly clear in his attitude towards the woman who was taken in adultery and was about to be stoned to death; and also in his attitude towards those who were putting him to death. He interceded on their behalf, and then asked not about answerability but responsibility for it.

Islamic theology is rooted in the concept merely of being answerable to. Man is answerable to God, which is a very narrow, legalistic idea. Sufism, a profound development within Islam, breaks away precisely from this idea of mere answerability and talks about responsibility for others. But is this simply a moralistic statement? Far from it. Sufism says: I am responsible for others, because the *other* and I constitute a common reality. There is an indissoluble bond between the *other* and me. Hence the Sufi emphasis on compassion and love. This is not merely a moralising stance but is rooted deeply in the awareness of a part of human nature. The same struggle takes place in the secularist ideologies. There, too, the legalistic idea prevails and the ethical idea of responsibility is submerged, but does not altogether disappear. I cannot go into greater detail but that is the first conclusion.

The second conclusion that can be drawn is that not only do the Semitic faiths and the secularist ideologies of the West not provide any coherent, systematic concept of Universal Responsibility, but they cannot. They cannot because they have surrounded the concept of Universal Responsibility with so many presuppositions of their own, and those presuppositions are not universally shared. They are shared only by those who believe in their faith or their particular ideology. So they cannot provide any genuine concept of universality.

It is in India, in the concepts of *dharma* and Bodhisattva, that we first find a systematic expression of Universal Responsibility. But, once again, both these ideas are surrounded by huge misconceptions. *Dharma* is taken to be religion, which it is not. It is presented as a Hindu concept which it most certainly is not. And the Bodhisattva is often perceived as a very likable fellow, a good human being, somebody like Prince Mishkin in Dostoievski's novel *The Idiot*, himself good but unable to change the world which is unjust and cruel. That is not what the Bodhisattva is. His Holiness has already gone into the question of the Bodhisattva ideal.

15

Dharma provides a genuine ground for Universal Responsibility because it is not surrounded by presuppositions of any kind. We do not have to believe even in the existence of God in order to respond to the 'other'. It is a response of the inner essence of our being in which the whole of reality is grounded. Hence the compassion. The *Mahabharata* says this again and again. Here is one quotation: "Even gods are unable to trace the footsteps of a man who, aware of his unity with all beings and having no goal for himself, works ceaselessly for their good."

Lastly, if all these wonderful ideas developed in India, and Buddhism is an extremely important part of Indian thought, then the question that we have to answer is: why is there a history of violence and hatred and the degradation of human worth in India, which persists to this day? It is quite clear that a mere recounting of the history of ideas will not do. We have to go much deeper into the problem and then remove the presuppositions which surround these ideas. It is in these presuppositions, I think, that the roots of violence lie. Only then can we rediscover the compassion and beauty that abound in human life.

MOHINDER SINGH: We have two very powerful models of progress, the Marxian model and the capitalist model. Ten years ago I would not have believed that the Marxian model could collapse so soon. But it has collapsed before our very eyes. Now only the capitalist model remains and those who agree with it are very happy that they have been able to destroy the Marxian model. However, this capitalist model will also collapse because it is not based on compassion and Universal Responsibility.

I have been asked to present the Sikh perspective on this issue. But what is the 'Sikh perspective'? It seems to me that even to claim a Sikh identity is a result of the degeneration of Sikhism. Guru Nanak spoke of a universal society based on compassion and Universal Responsibility. This degenerated into a movement with the passage of time, and so today I am called a Sikh. But Guru Nanak himself was not a Sikh. He came at a time when religions were in conflict with each other and with the State. Two movements provided the answer to this conflict, the Bhakti Movement and the Sufi Movement. Guru Nanak's answer was similar to that of these two movements—to transcend the conflict. The first words he uttered when he was enlightened were very significant: "Na Ko Hindu, na ko Musalman"—"I see no Hindu and no Muslim." Which is not to say that he had lost his eyesight, but that he had gained the vision whereby he could see beyond and transcend the narrow labels of Muslim and Hindu. I am sure if he were here today to see my turban he would say: "I see no Sikh."

What was his philosophy? I would like to sum it up in a few simple words: "Nam japna, Krit karna Vand Chakna"—"Pray, Work, Serve and Share." Here he is suggesting a universal model, always remembering God or meditating on God. What is Guru Nanak's God? It is not reducible to a Sikh God. Guru Nanak's teachings give us a picture of his model of godliness. He spoke of earning one's livelihood through pious means and sharing its fruit with others. It is here that this model is different from the Marxian model, which forces people to share what they have, not through their own free will. In the capitalist model they can make any amount of material progress, but there is no compassion, no concept of sharing. So here Guru Nanak is suggesting a model of sharing, but one based on freedom of choice. Once Guru Nanak was asked who was the better person, a Hindu or a Muslim. People waited anxiously for his answer. They thought that he might say Hindus were superior because he came from a Hindu background. But his answer was: "Shub karma bajo, donven nohi"—"Without good action, both are of no consequence to me." He emphasised that truth is high but higher still is truthful living.

Guru Nanak's model of society was that people would live together and none would own property. It would all be God's property. People would get up early in the morning and say their prayers after their ablutions, then go to work in the fields. Guru Nanak used to work in the fields even in his old age. After this, they would again bathe, meditate and then eat a meal in the community kitchen. They would say their prayers before going to sleep at the end of the day. Thus, a Sikh goes to sleep with God's name in his mind and gets up early in the morning only to repeat it again.

I am often asked about the two labels given to us, one by the western media—the fundamentalists—which we are not, and the other by the Indian media, I am sorry to say—the terrorists—which we also are not. I would like to emphasise that once a man is a terrorist he cannot be a Sikh, because in the teachings of the Guru there is no place for violence.

And which is the best religion? I remember being invited to a conference a year ago where this question was debated. I intervened and said that if we were to go by the people in that hall, since the majority were Christians they would say the best religion is Christianity. Outside, in Delhi, Hindus who were in the majority would say their religion is the best religion. Near Gurudwara Bangla Sahib, where Sikhs predominate, we would hear that Sikhism is the best religion. But, in fact, the Guru has provided the answer to this question: "Sarva Dharam Sreshtha Dharam, Har ko nam jap nirmal karam"—"Of all the religions the best religion is to remember God and do pious deeds." The Guru emphasised that there are various ways of realising the truth, not only the Sikh way. Our world is burning; show mercy and save it in whatever manner you can, not the 'Sikh' manner, the 'Hindu' manner or the 'Muslim' manner. This was the teaching that was given to us by Guru Nanak. Yet see what has happened to Sikhism. With the passage of time it has become institutionalised.

I often quote the following example: Guru Nanak started the concept of *dharamsala*, a place where *dharma* could be practised, which later came to be called a gurudwara. Guru Nanak's gurudwara was different from others and, interestingly, the first *dharamsala* was built by a man called Sajandi Thag who had been a robber in the past. He became Guru Nanak's first convert and started this first *dharamsala*, a place where those in need of shelter or food came and took it at any time of the day or night. Women in distress could also seek shelter there. That was the original concept of *dharamsala*. But what is the *dharamsala* today? A big Sikh temple with a big boundary wall around it, guarded by security men; a place that people fight over for control. The bigger the temple the greater the income accruing to it, and more bitter the fighting. I have never seen any fights in my own small temple where I live; it does not have any income. But there is a major battle over the Gurudwara Sis Ganj.

When I was invited to a big seminar at Khalsa College in Amritsar, I said: "Let me tell the truth. Over time, as Sikhism started developing as an institution, a Sikh code of conduct developed. Bhai Nand Lal laid down this Sikh code of conduct. That is very relevant: it was a Nand Lal and not a Nand Singh who

18

prescribed what is the right way of living as a Sikh, a model Sikh. He was a court poet of Guru Gobind Singh, and Guru Gobind Singh did not force him to become Nand Singh. So he was not forced to become a Sikh, nor to call himself 'Singh'. This was the model given by the Gurus. But, today, who defines a Sikh? A semi-religious body called the SGPC (Shiromani Gurudwara Prabhandak Committee). If my actions do not accord with their politics, they will declare me a renegade, and I can then be excommunicated by my community."

Guru Gobind Singh, the tenth Guru, said: "Manas ki jat sabe ek pahchanbo"—"Recognise that all of mankind is one." His followers imbibed this teaching. One such was Bhai Ghanaiya, who used to serve water to the people injured on the battlefield. One day, people reported to the Guru that one of his Sikhs was even serving water to the Muslims, the enemy. Guru Gobind Singh asked Bhai Ghanaiya for an explanation. He said very simply: "Master, you told me to recognise the whole of mankind as one and I have learnt your lesson very well." The Guru gave him boxes of ointments, saying: "After serving water to the enemy, you should also apply some ointment and balm to their wounds." This is the model that we should follow. Our answer is to seek guidance from the teachings of the Guru and not from the books of people such as myself and others.

FATHER T.K. JOHN: Dreams are a very important part of Indian philosophy, theology and mystical traditions. Therefore I would like to start with a dream. The very purpose of our coming together seems to be our desire to dream of a culture and civilisation where there is no gun, no lathi, no weapon; where there is no poverty, no crime, no fraud and deception; where there is no injustice and no hunger. This is our dream of a civilisation of love, a different future.

I think a gathering of minds and of hearts that share the same dream is crucial so that all the heritages of humanity can be brought together to heal our society of the diseases that afflict it. But it is not enough to dream. I refer to and represent one aspect of this heritage, that is the Christian tradition of compassion for the oppressed, where Jesus Christ becomes the crystallisation of that compassion, of that transcendental God.

It is not disembodied spirituality, nor idealism nor vision that will achieve anything, but the spirituality that is embodied and becomes the hands and the feet that act to remove the darkness and the filth from our history and our present-day lives. Thomas Merton, a great friend of His Holiness the Dalai Lama, refers to the significance of mystical experience and tradition and asks to become a purifying power to remove the filth from our human mind. Because there is physical suffering, there is mental suffering and there is spiritual suffering. Physical suffering is largely the creation of filthy minds, greed, oppression, dishonesty, fraud and so forth. Therefore, this can be removed only by the removal of mental suffering represented by greed, envy, jealousy, etc. Beyond that is a spiritual suffering, darkness, hopelessness and despair. Everyone wants to be happy, and to live in joy and bliss.

I conclude by referring to what the crystallisation of compassion means. According to the Christian tradition, it is the transcendental God becoming crystallised in the form of Jesus Christ. What did Jesus Christ do? He disrobed and wore ordinary clothes; he walked through paddy fields, market-places, through the woods and slums; he spoke in the language of the ordinary people; he touched the lepers, cleansed them and spoke with them. He did not hold himself apart from ordinary people and their problems. This should be our vision. Let us forget our animosities, the negative aspects of religion, culture and economic policies. Let ours become not a market economy, a free-for-all, but a civilisation of love and togetherness, where the sublimation and elevation of human nature can take place so that we can become human once again.

In other words, the heritage of humanity is to become a channel, a *dhara* of Akash Ganga, to initiate a *tapasya*, active *tapasya*, so that this Ganga can flow through our land once again, so that the women and men can become once again Woman and Man. In other words, a civilisation of love, a civilisation of compassion. Let this be the transcription of religions and ideologies for our time and our day. For that, my wish is that our hearts and hands will go forward in co-operation and committed action.

H.H. THE DALAI LAMA: I very much appreciate your frank and straightforward comments. As I mentioned earlier, my main concern is to promote the value of compassion and forgiveness among all people but particularly amongst those who do not subscribe to any formal faith, who are, so to speak, non-believers. When some-

20

one in ancient times talked about the value of compassion, which is the essence of Universal Responsibility, it was a useful idea although not as crucial as it is today when the situation is different.

In the economic sphere there is the North-South divide. For some time the North has only been concerned with its own future and has used every opportunity to exploit the poor countries. In the long term, because of the growing interdependence of our planet, those developed countries are facing problems themselves, including the degradation of the global environment, terrorism, illegal migration, etc. In order to solve the problem of the environment, the rich countries cannot demand of the poorer countries that they continue to live in poverty while the rich consume most of the earth's resources and create most of its pollution. We have to think of the human cost both for the poor and the rich. Because the rich control the global economy and produce most of the weapons, the problem cannot be solved unless they develop a sense of Universal Responsibility. They are beginning to realise that it is in their own interests to do so.

If your body is basically healthy and strong, any sickness that strikes you can be cured easily and quickly. But if you are unhealthy it becomes very difficult to cure you of disease. Similarly, if the whole planet is healthy, strong and stable, small problems can be solved easily. I often tell our western friends that they have a great deal of expertise in scientific and material things. Their knowledge is very good, but they have forgotten the intuitive understanding of the interconnectedness of all things, even though they are now rediscovering it in their research studies. There are great achievements in the field of knowledge but, looked at from another perspective, those horrible weapons are a product of the same knowledge. They bring immense suffering to humanity so from a human perspective they are very negative indeed, even while they are great achievements from a purely scientific point of view.

Genuine human co-operation cannot be brought about by force. It comes only when we realise that all of humanity is one—we are one human family. This planet is our only home. There is no real hope yet that we can migrate to other planets. It is very beautiful when poets describe the moon and stars, but if we were to go there we would find the environment very hostile. After a few centuries we may build a spacecraft and find some other suitable planet to live on but there is no such possibility in the foreseeable future. We must seriously take care of our planet before reality compels us to do so. These things emerge not only from a religious basis or a concept of morality. Being responsible for our planet, taking care of the whole world, is not a question of morality but a question of the needs of our own future. If we think deeply and from a wider perspective, we can get a clear picture.

This is the goal of true education. A sensitive and positive presentation of these problems which humanity is now facing needs to be cultivated amongst our young. I think we can solve the majority of our problems by developing a sense of Universal Responsibility. The various media have a great responsibility, and religion also has a very important role to play in this respect.

KAPILA VATSYAYAN: I hope all of you will agree that just as we have only this planet, so we also have only this day in which to reflect. Perhaps, therefore, we could avoid going into the basic tenets of religions, because we are all agreed about these. The predicament which faces us and of which His Holiness has reminded us, is the future of our whole planet and the compulsion, the sheer necessity, to be truly human. I think we do all understand that the original impulse of all religions is compassion and love and the distortions come with institutionalisation. I do not know the scientist's point of view as against the religious one, so let us listen to Prof. Ranjit Nair on this matter.

RANJIT NAIR: I am a philosopher of science and so, in some sense, I relate to science as a philosopher would. It has been very instructive to see the amount of consensus between representatives of the different religious traditions. This in itself is indicative of the special circumstances in which we find ourselves, and which have been profoundly elucidated by His Holiness the Dalai Lama. The fact is that from a situation where we were isolated communities, each adhering to its own laws, practices and usages, we have come together in a world which is easy of access, intimately connected, and where distances and time have shrunk. In such a situation it is inevitable to emphasise those traditions which have a positive bearing on the current situation. It is interesting that both Dr. Mohinder Singh and Dr. Badrinath Chaturvedi have stressed the enormous gap between actual professions of faith and their practice. This gap is probably permanent, in the sense that there is a role for a kind of critique, a moral critique, at any point in human history. All conceivable social arrangements will fall short of human felicity in some way or the other, not just yesterday or today but probably in the future too. Therefore, there must be a moral stand from outside, a transcendent standpoint if you like, which assesses social and ethical arrangements with a view to human felicity, and which is not tied to any contingent arrangement. There is a feeling that this world is inadequate, that this world's arrangements are inadequate and that we must strive for a better world.

It seems to me that this sense of moral perspective, or synoptic perspective, which looks not only at our particular predicament but at the predicaments of everyone is a kind of insight that our other traditions have brought to bear. It is one that is not reducible to our anthropological or biological heritage. I have come across this term as an expression of human-ness in the accounts of His Holiness the Dalai Lama and it seems to me this expression of human-ness must be something to be understood not in anthropological terms but in terms of this moral heritage; something that tries to reconstruct, at a reflective level, a kind of morality applicable to all societies and to all individuals, and that seeks to better human conditions. Fortunately, technology is on our side. Events are on our side and it seems more relevant than ever before to think in terms of a moral perspective that will not only address itself to the question of the relationship between man and environment which is, of course, a question of natural dependence, but also to the question of social dependence, the relationship between individual human beings and society.

RADHIKA HERZBERGER: You suggested that time was with us and that technology was with us. But I think we are in the present predicament largely because of the marriage of industry and technology, and the present degradation of the environment is closely related to that. Can there be a marriage between science and a less self-centered view of human nature? We see now that there is a marriage between science and industry and a consumer society, which seems to have won out the battle with Marxism.

23

RANJIT NAIR: I think the negative consequences of science and technology can be remedied through the social ideas that have been in the foreground, with the emphasis on democracy and enlightenment. Enlightenment professes universality and tolerance—Kant preached an ethics which was based on a condition of universality, for example. These things are intimately connected. One can provide the antidote for the other; and that is part of the potential of the philosophical tradition.

SUBHASH MALIK: I would just like to point out that we have been talking about love and compassion for 3,000 years. Is it working? The more we talk about it, the more it doesn't work. Isn't there something fundamentally wrong? It is not that our intentions are incorrect, but love and compassion are perhaps not the result of intention. Time, a temporal distance, is the inevitable consequence of the differentiation between thought and action, between intention and being. That temporal distance ensures in turn that compassion will not be. So whenever we propose something, do we not have to realise it in our lives immediately?

The problem is here, now, within us. It is not out there. Yet the tendency of all the sciences and all notions of knowledge has been to say that there is something out there that has to be solved tomorrow, in the future. The same thing is implied in the idea that there is an existential present, a past and a future. When time becomes the constant movement between the past and the future, the 'now' is forgotten. And what is that 'now'? The past and the future are our own creations from out of the 'now'. We only have fragmentary notions of the past, including of our own self. This 'now' does not begin with thought, but instead at that moment when all movement of thought stops, all thought ceases. It is an existential-experiential movement. Then something else starts operating. The knowledge of the past is only a sub-set of the larger universe in which and for which we are responsible. But do we take responsibility for our own self and our actions?

Do I take the responsibility for my own body, or do I say that someone else is responsible? How much do I know about my own body? A lot of fighting is going on inside it, as also on the outside. I do not take responsibility and I know very little about it. Yet I say this is mine. But can we really say that whatever is going on in the universe is ours? Is whatever is happening our responsibility? I think the starting point of responsibility is the stopping of all movement between the past and the future, because otherwise we are living in some unseen future, and in hope. These are very pious hopes, perhaps, but piety must begin now. When we are thirsty we want water right now. Our life depends on it; we do not talk about it. But when it comes to the question of love and compassion, we do not behave as if our lives depended on these qualities. Love and compassion need no discussion; this knowing belongs to the right brain, it begins now.

M.L. SONDHI: We have memories of 1959, of His Holiness arriving in India after the most unjust repression in Tibet, when freedom and democracy were crushed by the Chinese. We also know that today His Holiness advocates building a dialogue of moderation and compromise, building an Asian community. His Holiness has also advocated greater altruism in international relations.

Today we are trying to define Universal Responsibility, His Holiness' example notwithstanding, but we can only define it in terms of conflict resolution. Conflict resolution is in fact no resolution. A philosophy that involves the elimination of one party by another, of one State by another, or of one religion by another, cannot resolve any conflict. We have to go beyond the logic of contradiction to what the philosopher Basanta Kumar Malik has called the 'logic of mutual abstention'.

Whether it is the Marxists, the secularists or the scientists, all of whom tell us to be in the now and not in the past or in the future, they all adopt a reductionist analysis which leads to the fragmentation of the human being. Guru Gobind Singh says: "Jin Prem Kiyo Tin he Prabhu Payo"—"Only he who loves his fellow humans finds God." Human beings are very complex and multi-dimensional, and each one is subject to his or her own causal relations. Yet, because of something higher—whether it is Bodhisattva or God or whatever creative unity it is—the many become one.

Human beings are equipped with an integrative faculty. I do not have to quote Paul Tillich who calls it 'depth dimension' in human life; this totality of life was talked of long ago in the *Rig Veda*. And so His Holiness' philosophy, as I understand it, is that we cultivate an integrated approach to human nature, and reject the unending chain of action and reaction.

The trouble with Stalin, Lenin, Mussolini and Hitler and maybe others, too, was this continuous chain of action and reaction, resulting in the loss of the human being. I think the daily practice which His Holiness referred to is the daily renewal of this human-ness. Ramakrishna Paramahansa used to say that one must scrub the pot daily. But we live schizophrenic lives today because the total picture of the human being is lost. To regain this integration, we must not make a break with the past, as has just been advocated. This does not help us resolve conflict. The only method to resolve conflict is to transcend the difference between individuals, which itself is only possible if we believe that all life is sacred.

His Holiness does not offer us any instant remedy, whereas perhaps the Marxists do. He is asking for an integration of the partial views of human nature, of human life.

KAPILA VATSYAYAN: I thought I would just recall a session with J. Krishnamurti when we were discussing harmony, peace and violence, and a lot of intellectual arguments began. I cannot forget the smile with which he said, "But the violence is already here!" I hope we can avoid that violence.

FR. T.K. JOHN: I would like to mention that when he visited Agra in 1956, His Holiness named my young daughter Dickyi Chozin, the meaning of that name being 'intense religious happiness'. This morning his theme has been happiness. It is our responsibility to create happiness for all individuals on this earth. We as Indians advocate total nuclear disarmament. A worthy aim indeed. But we refuse to talk with our own neighbours about a nuclear-free zone. This, I think, is not consistent with our professed support of the total abolition of nuclear armaments. After all, we can move to that goal step by step.

BADRINATH CHATURVEDI: I see an all-enveloping quality in compassion, an ideal of all religions, but I think we have to devote ourselves to some critical questions. The first is the question of science. What is its religion? I think that has ceased to be an issue, by and large, whereas it might have been in the 19th century or early 20th century.

Today we are concerned more with the question of how religion has been taken over by politics or politicians. We are also asking why science, which was at one time an instrument of

26

war and destruction on a large scale, has also become an instrument of the slow poisoning and destruction of the ecological balance, and so on. Again, as regards religion, we talk of individual meditation. Religion is supposed to be something personal. But if it is supposed to be personal, why should it be called 'self-centred'? Yet when it becomes social or is institutionalised, all the evils and dysfunctionalities creep in. So how can we find some antidote or counteracting force to this tendency?

The other point to which I draw your attention has been mentioned in the proposition of the Foundation, to which His Holiness also made a reference. How should one impart education for rights of citizenship, for togetherness, for better living? What can be done so that education instills a sense of social responsibility in individuals, which transforms itself into social commitment? This social commitment then takes up issues of universal concern, such as those mentioned by His Holiness i.e., the question of survival and the question of happiness. Basically, at the root of all this is compassion or, as was mentioned by Prof. Sondhi, the question of conflict resolution, peace research, disarmament—as well as the dichotomy and ambivalence of external disarmament, pointed out by Dr. John.

SHARAT KUMAR: What really matters is action, inward and outward. Inward action means thinking out of our own mind and cleansing it. As we heard from His Holiness, all success in the external world also depends on the purity of our own mind. Then we need a technology for investigating our own mind about which we know very little. Also, what matters is to watch the gulf between our words and our actions. There are few who 'practise what they preach'. Practice is always at an individual level, and all action lies there. Meditation as a technology is perhaps useful for thinking over what we did during the day. Could we have done it a little better? Did we cause any harm to anyone? Could we achieve the same result without being aggressive, without pandering to our ego, without getting lost in our conflicting flow of thoughts? If we can look at ourselves in this way every day, perhaps we can learn to act much better to achieve all the success we long for, and that is what really matters. I think there is a great need to find a technique for opening the inner world of our mind.

KAPILA VATSYAYAN: I do not think that I have the courage to sum this up. I would like merely to mark a milestone so that we can go on to the next section. The question of what constitutes the 'I' in the sense of the self has come up in different ways. The self is the physical self, the body, in the sense of understanding whatever is happening inside. The outer self can be defined variously as environment, society, institution, ideology, movements, or what we call civilisation. This brings us back to the initial statements made by His Holiness today—what is Universal Responsibility, and the actor or the self as beginner of the inner responsibility? I would like once again to request His Holiness to perhaps make one or two observations on what has been said here about the dichotomy between thought and action, between individual, society and religion.

H.H. THE DALAI LAMA: Thought and action are two separate things, yet intimately connected. The action of human beings, particularly of those who are serious about what they do, usually comes from thought with a certain motivation. Then the action follows. So the effectiveness of thought emanates from action, but that action comes from thought and motivation. In a way it is very difficult to draw a distinction between the two; to know from one particular action in isolation whether it is positive or negative.

Human nature is such that we can change the future. However, as society or the community involves a combination of individuals, there is no possibility of bringing new ideas into the community or of changing the community's view of things unless initiatives come from individuals. Therefore, everything depends on individual action. I believe that in the foreseeable future religion at least will remain a very influential force and an important factor. Religion has its own technology or techniques. Like all human activities, religion can become destructive unless human feelings are involved, in the same way as science and technology can. Today both science and technology have destructive powers. There is nothing wrong with technology itself, nor with religion—only with the human thought that directs it. If we use our minds in wrong ways then they become destructive, and if they are used properly they have immense potential for the good of huma

Society Today: The Anatomy of Fragmentation
Chairperson: Sashi Kumar

SUDHIR KAKAR: While reading the very thoughtful paper by His Holiness entitled *A Human Approach To World Peace* which serves as the basis for our discussions, I was struck by a theme he repeats in different contexts. He states it succinctly when he says, "Whether a conflict lies in the field of politics, business or religion, an altruistic approach is frequently the sole means of solving it." He goes on to remind us that in conflicts we tend to forget the basic human nature which unites us, and asks the question why we do not pursue the altruistic approach more often.

My very brief remarks will seek to answer the question in the context of today's society. They pertain to the question of basic human nature raised by His Holiness but, of course, as this nature is visualised by my own professional orientation, that is by my partial view.

First, let me say that our basic human nature not only unites but also divides, the most important division being within ourselves. This division is an inevitable consequence of growing up from infancy to adulthood. Human nature is not only peaceful but also violent, not only compassionate but also impelled by possessive desires. In modern societies, because of the psychological revolution of the last hundred years, we have come to accept, however grudgingly, the fact of the divided self; even though we may continue to wish this division away, in the eminently human striving to have within us a unity of intent and purpose.

We have a greater appreciation today of the role of instinctual impulses that propel our behaviour. We do not seek to quell our passions through coercion by the community nor by the represen- tatives of morality within us. Or, at least, we do not do so with the same degree of ruthlessness as in some earlier periods. By understanding our instinctual nature, by showing it compassion, we hope to learn to integrate it better, so that it enriches our individual and collective lives. However, there is one major part of human nature, one of its greatest motivators, which is still regarded with moralistic horror. I am referring to human narcissism or self-love, the part of our nature which, if it remained at a primitive infantile level, would sabotage all altruism. Just as non-violence cannot be built by suppressing our aggression, altruism cannot be built on a denial or suppression of narcissism.

Compassion can only be achieved through a long, painful struggle with the passion of self-love, only by cultivating greater tolerance for narcissism in ourselves and in others. That is, it is only through a greater honesty about individual and collective motives that we can hope to turn primitive narcissism into its mature form. For there is a mature, healthy narcissism that provides the fuel for our ambition and purposes for the enjoyment of our activities and is critical in maintaining important aspects of our self-esteem. Without this maturation, self-love will remain at an infantile level and be expressed in such narcissistic perversions as smug superiority, arrogant self-righteousness or a sense of personal grandiosity.

Today, for many social and historical reasons, the constraints on the expression of primitive narcissism do not function quite as effectively. The divide between our narcissism and altruism is especially wide. Appeals to the ethic of altruism will not help in bridging this gulf. Only a mature narcissism can turn us away from the blinding of infantile self-love so that we can see the 'other'. We cannot develop the capacity for empathy without being able to see the 'other', and this empathy is the basis for altruism. We can then learn to look at conflict between individuals and groups in a more discriminating manner and not condemn them equally. There can be a mature, competitive aggressiveness directed at others who stand in the way of our cherished goals. Or there can be a narcissistic rage which erupts against those who are felt to threaten the basis of our individual or group-self. The first leaves no residue and the second smoulders on in an animosity which erupts periodically. The first does not stand in the way of the altruistic approach, the second makes it impossible.

In conclusion, I would have liked to say that my remarks are solely informed by my discipline, whereas the paper of His Holiness grows out of ethical concerns. Psychology is inscriptive while ethics is prescriptive. The former deals with what is in human nature, the indicative mood, whereas the paper emphasised what ought to be, the imperative mood. My statements depend for their validity on verification: are they correct? Whereas ethical statements depend on justification: do they conduce to the good? But alas, such distinctions can never be made in any statement about human beings. There is always an intermingling and intertwining of empirical endeavour and ethical and moral presuppositions, sometimes overt and sometimes covert, with all the conflicts and judgments this entails for every one of us.

I hope His Holiness does not mind if I include him in our common humanity and our inevitable blending of the 'is' with what 'ought to be'.

M.B. ATHREYA: Those of you who know me as a student of management may wonder what I am doing here. But that illustrates the problem of Universal Responsibility—the tendency that we have of putting labels on each other; religious, linguistic and professional labels are the latest of these. In my growth as an individual I have tried to resist excessive specialisation. As I read more about management and look at management in all walks of life, I am led to suggest that the Universal Responsibility theme may be extended into considering what kind of contribution each one of us can make in universal management. At the moment, there is universal drift, universal mismanagement. There has to be some kind of collective human management of resources, of people and so on, perhaps even going beyond the world of human beings and living things to something like cosmic management. There is no limit to Universal Responsibility.

One of the reasons why Universal Responsibility has been on the decline is that we have lost our wholeness, our integration, our totality. Some familiarity with Sanskrit makes me turn to the concept of *purna, purnatva*. But before we can understand this concept of undiminishing wholeness, before we can look at the world as a whole, we as individuals have to become whole. We have to be aware of the splintering that is taking place internally;

we need to understand this in terms of the altruism that His Holiness has talked about and the two kinds of altruism that Sudhir talked about. How does this altruism manifest in actual behaviour, in the world of managing oneself and things? Perhaps the only test of altruism is not whether a person feels altruistic, but whether he actually takes a unilateral initiative for the larger good.

That gets us into other issues, such as why we have ceased being responsible towards those who are weaker. We have no difficulty in being responsible to those who are stronger and more aggressive than us. Do we wait for a period of mutual abstention? Or can one side take the initiative and convert the other? These are not easy conflicts to resolve. I think we are facing the dangers of divisiveness. In a way, even the last session's discussion and our academic dialogues amongst intellectuals or among voluntary agencies, where people are certainly even more dedicated than in other walks of life, show that there is a tendency to brand ideas. Within religion there is further splintering. There is no end to the tendency to splinter. There are Shias and Sunnis, Akalis and Nirankaris, Freudian psychology and Jungian psychology, Japanese management and American management. Can we avoid this splintering?

The simplistic route of denying differences will not lead us towards Universal Responsibility. The challenge is how to stay differentiated but with respect for each other, how to acknowledge our own differentiation and identity, and also that of others, and totally resist these tendencies towards domination. Here *advaita* in practice seems to offer a valuable idea, that I have my personal responsibility but at the same time I represent the universal soul of Brahman and, therefore, I need to take responsibility for the entire universe. Western social science also deals with this problem. There is the problem of alienation due to mass urbanisation. There is less of a sense of owning things and, therefore, less responsibility within large organisations. There is a breakdown of norms, which is partly the consequence of the disappointment that the citizen feels in brutalised politics, sluggish government, non-competitive business. Even voluntary organisations are occasionally driven by rivalry and inner conflicts.

We also have a diffusion of identity. People have great difficulty in defining themselves and are consequently very much open to manipulation by someone who offers them an aggressively narrow identity. We have difficulty dealing with short, transient authority relationships. Although the world's wealth has increased and the output of goods and services has increased, we remain deprived. We have been excessively dependent upon science, but it has to become more and more people's science rather than mega-science. We have grown too dependent on the State. Therefore, the kind of initiative (undertaken here) is very important. We need the meeting of the world's five billion minds, possibly through representatives in some way, on these kinds of issues.

It would perhaps be more relevant to us in this room to look at the eastern analysis. There was a time when all religions propounded that people be in touch with God, whether this was seen as an anthropomorphic concept or as some principle of energy, some kind of cosmic awareness. It is reflected in various ways in the beautiful verses that Mr. Mohinder Singh quoted. The Shanti Maha Mantra, I suggest, is a mantra which is worth memorising, to be recited frequently. It is a fantastic anticipation of ecological, environmental and inter-planetary issues. It prays for peace for all things and beings, in all ways. The mantra's premise is that peace is indivisible. We cannot have only partial responsibility because the word 'responsibility' then loses its meaning.

We have lost a sense of perspective and balance in our life goals. What is the purpose of life? What is the meaning of life? Eastern philosophy traditionally provided certain answers. We need to come back to this *dharma* or righteousness as the touchstone for anything which we intend to do. I do not know much more about *dharma*, but just to go into the injunction of not only non-violence in deed but in word and in thought seems an important step. We have got caught up with *artha*, wealth, by any means, the pursuit of materialism. We have also lost sight of a meaningful model of the entire life cycle, the *Jeevashrams—brahmacharya, grahastha, vanaprastha* and *sanyasa*. The latter two expressions *vanaprastha* and *sanyasa* are totally unfamiliar to a modern educated mind which is caught in its own cycle. There is a decline of the *gunas* in human beings—the modern world is caught in cycles of *rajas* and *tamas: satva* is almost lost. The modern world is feverish, passionate, energetic, active, becomes exhausted and

33

docile for a while, then re-awakens, but at no point is there peace, *shanti*, or stability.

The ancients divided all knowledge into *vidya* and *brahma-vidya*. The first is the knowledge of material objects and things. The second is more important than this, since *brahma-vidya* attempts a deeper, more fundamental knowledge. The knowledge of the self that modern psychology also attempts to arrive at was part of ancient philosophy, which tried to understand human nature and gave us various ways in which the self-development process can take place—through analysis, meditation, introspection and daily practice. But we suffer today from *avidya*, ignorance. *Dharma*, we think, is for the impractical; we think we cannot survive in this world if we talk about and practise *dharma*. Yet Universal Responsibility eventually comes back to *dharma*. There are inevitably some elites in every society, and I suggest that these elites, the *shreshtas*, have failed in their role model of exhibiting *dharma* which would then enable others to follow them.

In terms of action, I think *dharma* has to be implemented not through governments nor through legislation, but through mass education and participative action campaigns. We have to create several little eddies of this kind of conscious, universally responsible action around the world. I would also suggest that we move towards what we are already doing in India and create an international worldwide network of non-governmental organisations; not against somebody, not against government, UN agencies, prisoners, academia and the like, but a benign, facilitating, catalyst network of NGOs.

We do need laws and regulations to an extent. The world is made up of institutions and systems which will transcend the nation states. I think all loyalties to religion, the nation, the corporation, are in some ways inevitable, but these are also dangerous for Universal Responsibility. We have to find some way of civilising and moderating, by finding other institutions and processes.

I think all of us will agree that no place of worship should be destroyed—to take the very concrete, specific and current issue of the Babri Masjid; and we should forswear any form of conversion to our point of view, faith or institution that uses direct or indirect coercion of any form. We should renounce all forms of violence—

comparatively differentiated brand-marketing is also a kind of intellectual and spiritual violence. Would bureaucrats, professors and college principals be able to take pleasure in the success of other such organisations and offer them their support and networking? Can we ourselves eliminate our destructive tendencies? If so, I think Universal Responsibility will be manifested.

M.J. AKBAR: We really have two themes for our Panel. The first is 'Universal Responsibility' and the second, the sub-theme, is 'The Anatomy of Fragmentation'. The question that arises is this: what is the difference between the 'universe' and the 'world'? The term 'universe' has, I think, been chosen with care. Obviously, when we speak of a universal sense of responsibility, or Universal Responsibility, we do not mean that we are going to get into spaceships and create a sense of responsibility in all the worlds that exist in our universe. What, then, is the specific meaning of the word 'universe' within the context of our discussion today? It is not just a world that we live in plus a few stars. In my view the word 'universe' has been used because it means 'world plus faith'. It means 'world plus mystery'; it thus refers to both the micro-level, including our inner sense of our soul, and the macro-level, the human world as we understand it. But the human world is called a universe only because it draws attention to the *atma* or the soul, from which we have to find the energy to address this particular problem. We all of us live in both worlds simultaneously, but the share of attention which each world demands from us changes at different periods in history.

The biggest casualty of human experience in the last 200 years has been faith. The great determinants of human thought and action in that period have been materialism, industrial production and nationalism. These are ideas that have controlled human progress in the sense not of human growth or evolution but in that they have led certain parts of the world to take command of certain other parts. We can subdivide the world in two ways. One is the economic categorisation of the world, which is familiar—the First World, the Second World, and the Third World of poor nations. But there is yet another categorisation. We are in a state of change, particularly now, and I have a feeling that we have to evolve towards a new understanding of ourselves. I submit that that understanding goes back to an earlier categorisation of the world, in terms of belief systems—such as the Christian world, the Hindu, Buddhist, Marxist and Islamic worlds. But at one level these worlds are set against each other, in terms of the psychological and the intellectual. We must also address this problem.

Religion is essentially founded on the fear of the unknown, the mystery of birth and death. Answers are sought either through belief or through exercising the human intellect, or through belief in the message as a source of information and faith. But religion has this advantage, that while it seeks to answer questions about the fear of the unknown, it also gives us great strength to deal with our fear of the known, the fear of the material world. In this context, faith actually creates the impetus for scientific inquiry, because such inquiry is impossible without the ingredient of faith. It is only when we are not afraid of the known that scientific inquiry becomes possible.

His Holiness has referred to the need for *ahimsa* at some length. But *ahimsa* is not so much the issue as *bhay*. This is the age of fear and, therefore, the need of the time is not so much for *ahimsa* as for *abhay*. *Ahimsa* will flow from *abhay*, not the other way round. *Abhay* is the appropriate word, being an abstract noun meaning fearlessness, the quality of fearlessness. *Nirbhay* implies a subject possessed of this quality—(s)he or that which is fearless.

Therefore, we must first address ourselves to the reasons for fear in large numbers of people, and also in the individual in his relationship to his immediate community and his wider world, to his gods, to his inner intellectual and psychological world. Also, after we have addressed the individual sense of fear, we have to address the community sense of fear, then the national sense of fear. I submit that the Christian world is without faith but is in command of the economy; the Hindu-Buddhist world is characterised by withdrawal—it does not participate in the real sense of the word; the Marxist world is in a shambles and is suffering from defeat; and the Islamic world at the moment is characterised by a sense of revenge against history. Perhaps 'revenge' is not the most appropriate word. But how else does one explain the spirit of Iqbal searching for an answer to his *shikwa*—searching for an answer to his complaint to God at its having been left behind on earth?

Over the last 200 years the two great pillars of Islamic confidence—political confidence and the confidence of faith—which were translated into the political path as the Ottoman Empire and the Mughal Empire have both now collapsed, leaving a residual impact that was followed by Christian imperialism. Has this resulted in a crisis of political confidence and of faith? The problem between the Jews and the Arabs would disappear and there would be peace tomorrow if the Arabs could be convinced that Israel is not an outpost of Christian imperialism. The perception of Israel as an enemy is an extension of the perception of Christian imperialism; in that sense the Crusades go on and they will go on unless linkages between Israel and its mother of command ideology are ended. Strangely, the discussions at peace conferences address issues which have no relevance to the reality of the Middle East, to mind-sets which are at war and are totally different. The mind-set of the energies that Saddam Hussein created was on a totally different plane from George Bush's and was irrespective of the past, present and future of Saddam. The inspirational power that he derived for a period of about two weeks, which gave him legitimacy in certain parts of the world, was created out of a totally different mind-set from George Bush's. Therefore, victory and defeat in that war are meaningless and have no relevance to reality. Something very significant was missing from the latest peace conference in Madrid, which was the Islamic Umma. We will not achieve peace without a dialogue with the Umma, however many treaties are signed. Nor is peace possible in the absence of fearlessness. Fear destabilises what exists and simultaneously constructs identities.

Two words that are very relevant here, because they are the crux of the political battles today, are 'majority' and 'minority'. But what is a majority and what is a minority? Are the Muslims a minority? At what stage of this long and complex relationship between the Muslims of the subcontinent did they become a minority? Were they a minority when Mohammed Ghazni was attacking Sind, when Mohammed Gori was defeating Prithvi Raj, when Khilji and Malik Qafoor had achieved a magnificent feat of arms and reached the south? Were the Muslims a minority under the Sultanate? Under the

Moghul empire? Certainly not. So minority status is not a reflection of demography. Equally, it is not an extension of economic status. No one can maintain that there were no poor Musalmans during the Moghal empire, nor that there are no poor Hindus today. In fact, most of the Bajrang Dal activists are poor. The majority-minority syndrome has nothing to do with population and it has nothing to do with hunger. What it has to do with is fear.

Any group of people who feel afraid in a society become a minority, no matter what their numerical or economic strength. Fear defines a minority. Therefore, if we want to address the problem of minorities, we have to address the problem of fear. Because we had been conditioned to think of Musalmans as the only minority group, we were completely surprised when we discovered that, in a certain year, we had converted Sikhs into a minority. We were more taken aback still when we discovered that in a certain other year we had converted the Assamese into a minority. And we are going to be terribly surprised in 50 years' time when we discover that we have created a minority of our tribals, when they also start asking for their rights, for their liberation from the Indian nation. Actually, nobody is asking for liberation from the Indian Union and Indian nation—what is really being asked for is liberation from fear. And when groups of people from Pourulia, Jharkhand right up to Maharashtra and through the great heart of India seek their liberation from fear, and they will do so, we will still not know how to deal with them because we are not addressing ourselves to the real problem, which is fear.

Unfortunately fear seems to be one of the ties that bind in our unhappy world—not merely in our domestic environment, but also between national and world identities and the world community. Neo-colonialism is nothing but the continuous export of fear. For me the obverse of fear is calm. I have heard His Holiness' beautiful description that happiness is only the extension of the present. This is the moment to be happy, right now. Happiness of the past is but a memory. Happiness of the future is just a wish. And, yet, a little later he added that the present itself was so infinitesimal that it could not really be experienced. If we were to use the purely deductionist approach, would we then say that happiness is impossible? But we are blessed by the fact that, inexpressible though it may be, happiness does exist.

SASHI KUMAR: Before we invite responses from the Panel, I would like to add another dimension which has been troubling me personally. When we discussed the concept of the anatomy of fragmentation, or heritage in terms of Universal Responsibility, it struck me as a discourse of this forum that we are living in a post-Marxist dispensation, the crumbling of the socialist world as a kind of given, and we do not have to worry any more about that. We were also talking about the need for compassion, altruistic compassion, which Dr. Kakar qualified as only being able to come out of a wholesome narcissistic notion and a total understanding of ourself, which is then extended to others in our environment. It strikes me as strange that one of the greatest doctrines in my opinion—and I refer here to Marxism—should receive such short shrift for precisely the distortions of which religion stands accused.

There have been many more wars, deaths and distortions, and much more destruction in the name of religion than in the name of ideology. Admittedly, the culprit is not religion *per se* but religion in its distorted manifestation. Does this mean that religion has been appropriated by the rulers, or by those who want to inflict their sense of power over others? We have also seen in history the phenomenon of the oppressed becoming the oppressors at a particular point in time, as is happening in the socialist world today. The oppressed who gained power became the oppressors: I make no apology for the distortion of the system nor of ideologies, nor can I be an apologist for the bureaucratisation of the system, of the standardisation which is sought to be enforced from above. His Holiness mentioned motivation as the most crucial factor. Would not the motivation of a system of thought or ideology like Marxism be seen as initially and intrinsically humane? It may be seen as the need to bring egalitarianism to the system, a reaction to a kind of feudal dispensation, and to resolve the problems created by the vitiated system that religion gave us at one time.

Secondly, we are living too close to the history of the 'collapse of Marxian ideology or Marxism' to decide obits in this meeting. I would not like to be seen as a Marxist speaking in this forum, but it appears short-sighted to me, and certainly not a considered statement, to say that the time is opportune for the realisation of a new spirituality—in terms of Universal Responsibility—because we have a congenial set-up and because the socialist states have collapsed and totalitarian regimes have collapsed. That they have collapsed is a very good thing. Whether a new ideology will emerge from that remains to be seen.

RAFIQ ZAKARIA: I do not agree with the remark that there have been more wars fought in the name of religion than for any other cause. In medieval times when religion was the dominant idea, it was no doubt exploited by forces on either side at the cost of the other; it was used to whip up emotions and to misuse power. But there have been wars even after religion ceased to be a dominant factor. The First and Second World Wars were not fought in the name of religion; they were fought in the name of liberty and they resulted in the massacre of many more human beings than all the wars in history put together. There have also been conflicts in the name of democracy, with the leftists claiming that they represent the people, while the western forms of democracy denounce them as traitors to the cause and upholders of dictatorship. It seems people need some slogan to fight for and with, and there are enough selfish leaders to provide it to them. The world would, indeed, be a better place to live in if they were moved by compassion instead.

The Prophet of Islam hated aggression of any kind; he was no war-monger. He was defending himself rather than being the aggressor in all the wars that he fought or was forced to fight. According to most western writers, not more than 500 people were killed in all his wars, and in the last one, according to the orientalists themselves, less than 20 people were killed. These seem like minor skirmishes because our wars today mean the death of millions and the uprooting of many more millions which did not happen in the past.

M.J. Akbar has made a good point about fear being the negation of the spirit of accommodation. He is right; fear creates a ghetto mentality among the oppressed, while the oppressors try to keep them under control. This is how the wall of fear is built, and has been so throughout history. There is talk of American imperialism, Russian imperialism. Ironically, our neighbours are even talking of Indian imperialism, out of their fear because they are smaller than us. We are the majority and they are the minority. But what is the solution to this? Nobody has given a clear answer as to how to remove this fear, which strikes at the very root of human relationships.

M.J. AKBAR: Certain things are the job of a clever analyst and certain things are the responsibility of wisdom. I would really like to hear His Holiness' answer on the subject of fear.

H.H. THE DALAI LAMA: The source of conflict or unhappiness is fear. But I would like to ask, what is justice? What is truth? Different faiths do have conceptions and definitions of truth and justice. But for ordinary human beings without any religion or involvement in religion or ideology, what is justice? Animals have no religion yet, generally speaking, they respond favourably when we treat them honestly. If we show them anger or hostility they respond accordingly. So even animals appreciate kindness and honesty. We humans also have a natural tendency to appreciate someone who is honest and compassionate towards us, who tells the truth fully and openly, and we respond positively to such a person.

M.J. AKBAR: My understanding of justice would be freedom from exploitation. I do not think we can claim that all human beings will equally be able to achieve whatever they have to achieve in society. There will be imbalances, according to genes, education and environment. Everyone will not be equal and everybody is not going to be equally happy nor equally comfortable. But justice is a practical working relationship for the management of society; justice is a tool for the preservation of peace. It can only be there if there is no perception of exploitation from a certain specific ideology that we hold; if we are not subject to exploitation regardless of which stratum we are born into. The absence of oppression for me would be the best definition of justice.

H.H. THE DALAI LAMA: I think your concept of justice concerns society or a social being, and that is one kind of justice. But more generally, what is the concept of truth? Is there any difference between truth and justice? I do not know. My precise question is, what is truth?

M.J. AKBAR: It is one's own understanding, because each man's truth is different.

H.H. THE DALAI LAMA: But what is the meaning of truth?

AMRIK SINGH: We are treating religion as only an ideology, but religion is more than that. It is therefore incorrect to consider only one aspect of religion and overlook the significance of the other aspects. Further, religion historically has been a profoundly humanising factor or influence. The 'good old days' witnessed a great deal of barbarity and violence. Today's violence and barbarity can indeed be traced to religious conflict, but that is not the only expression of religion, nor is violence the result only of religious strife.

Mr. Zakaria spoke about the two World Wars and the devastation they brought. These wars were not fought because of religion but, as Mr. Akbar pointed out, for industrial, economical and political supremacy. In today's world, conflict and war ultimately can be traced to militarisation at one level or another. This militarisation has come about not because of religion but because of other factors. Let us therefore adopt a more carefully considered reaction to what religion has done or can do. I think we should also consider the polarity pointed out by Sudhir Kakar in regard to narcissism and compassion. That is a level of discussion which needs to be taken into account as well and not ignored.

SUBHASH MALIK: May I comment on a point made by Mr. Akbar? Dr. Zakaria's intervention has made it unnecessary for me to repeat the point that wars have more frequently been fought in other names than religion. But to his point that fear is a source of fragmentation, may I suggest that fear can also be self-generating? Why should communities feel that they are minorities and generate fear within themselves? A community, minority or otherwise, exists in a world of relationships with other similar communities and with the total community of which it is a part. These relationships must be expressed through gestures towards each other, towards the larger, more heterogeneous community. It is the lack of this attitude, rather than an illusory and self-induced fear, which intensifies fragmentation.

H.H. THE DALAI LAMA: Let us return to the idea of truth. Perhaps, as reality and appearance are two different things, so also are truth and untruth. Sometimes appearance and reality synchronise, they are the same. That then is truth, or this is how I understand the meaning of truth. Therefore, when we interact with society or with our family members or the community generally, there is no need for fear if we develop relationships on the basis of truth by being open and sincere. If we pretend to be something and in reality we are something else, suspicion develops and that creates fear. When we understand the value of truth, there is not much difference between the needs of a majority or minority community, even though the numbers vary a lot; for truth is always truth. So if we consider the importance of truth then that eventually reduces misunderstanding, doubt and fear.

In order to develop that commitment to truth we develop compassion, which comes from a deep respect for the rights of others. I have no right to cheat anybody and I will be very unhappy if someone cheats me. Similarly, the people I cheat will also be unhappy. So, you see, when I appreciate their rights, that automatic feeling or tendency to cheat, or to say something and mean another, disappears. Therefore, altruism and compassion develop through a commitment to the truth. We come to truth through compassion. We can develop healthier relations with individuals as well as with the community, and that automatically reduces fear. That is my belief, my opinion. Fear is the most dangerous destroyer of our happiness.

SUBHASH MALIK: We have been talking of the anatomy of fragmentation. But we are still talking in external terms, in terms of East and West and in terms of all the other conceptual models existing at the present time. The anatomy of fragmentation, as I understand it, is something like this: here is a man driving a bus, and the bus is constantly having accidents. We repair the bus, we replace the bus. But the real problem is that the driver is drunk.

The human brain is in disorder because only a part of it functions, because a fragment of the human brain is in conflict. There is no eastern pain, there is no western pain; there is just pain. I may know that I am fragmented and yet I say that thought itself is fragmented. The intellect is fragmented in order to understand reality, but it can then understand only the reality which is experienced. It is like a cricket commentary: the commentary is taken to be a reality. The problem today is that we are not in touch with the experiential side of man. If I am unintegrated, it is impossible for me to create an integrated world. But it is important to accept the fact that I am unintegrated. Likewise with the acceptance of fear. It has to be experienced. It cannot be washed away. So perhaps, as a first step, all we can do is to acknowledge and understand fully our fragmentation, just as it is important to understand, experience and acknowledge our fear.

I shall finish with two anecdotes. Firstly, there was a man walking in search of truth, and behind him was the devil and his friend. The man bent down and picked up something. The friend told the devil that the man had picked up the truth, and that he was going to gain freedom. And the friend asked the devil what he was going to do about that. The devil said: "Don't worry, friend, I am going to help him organise it."

My second tale is of two monks, an older one and a younger one, who were out walking one day. They came to a river where a woman was standing, wanting to cross over it. So the older monk picked up the woman and took her across. As they continued on their way, the younger monk said to the older one: "Sir, we are told in our scriptures not to touch a woman. But you touched that woman back there. Why did you do that?" He replied: "I picked her up because she needed to cross the river, but I dropped her long ago. You are still carrying her with you."

ANOTHER SPEAKER: The discussion about fear tended to become a bit philosophical. It reminded me of a statement made by a psychoanalyst, I think it was Laing, who said that there is a word in the English language to describe somebody who feels he is being persecuted—that word being 'paranoid'. But there is no word to describe someone who feels he is being persecuted and is in fact being persecuted. What emerges from this is that the concept of fear is not something purely psychological. It is grounded in a sense of heteronomy, or loss of autonomy, and this in turn depends on contingent social conditions. It is not sufficient to tell somebody who has a sense of the fear of oppression that he must eliminate it. The removal of fear is conditional upon removing those very circumstances which create the fear.

SUDHIR KAKAR: I think a distinction needs to be made between fear and panic. Fear is a very normal experience for communities.

It is when fear becomes panic, which means it overtakes all of our personality, that it becomes dangerous. It is not possible to eliminate fear. That is part of the human condition, of communities; at various historical times they experience fear. It is when fear turns into panic that it becomes a problem.

Universal Responsibility in Action: Reclaiming the Whole
Chairperson: Sanjit (Bunker) Roy

LUKAS HENDRATA: I am from UNICEF, which means that I am an international bureaucrat, and that means going the furthest distance you can imagine from philosophy. So what I am going to share with you may not be very profound. We have been talking about fear. I think fear is involved when we are faced with the task of translating what we believe into action. The danger of meetings or forums like ours is that we tend to agree too easily. It is easy to agree at the level of concepts. But when it comes down to the actual realisation of these ideas, when it comes to actually translating these concepts into action, we need to be very careful. In particular, we need to be very careful when dealing with the problem of the role of religion in the conduct of public business. I will use the term 'public square'.

The public square is a forum in which we all are contributing to society with ideas and concepts on how government could function. We often hear that since we are a secular society, we cannot bring religion and religiously grounded values into the public square. We often hear that secularism means the separation of church and State, which means the separation of religion and religion-based moral values from the public realm. In his book Justice Iyer wrote that the idea of secularism is the effective separation of religious and temporal matters, with the State being kept out of the former and God being kept out of the latter.

I believe this is too simplistic a definition of secularism. To begin with, I wonder if anyone can keep God out of anywhere! To attempt this is to attempt to render the public square naked, short of any moral or religious value. We think that the naked public square is a safe place. However, history proves otherwise. Once the public square is not clothed with meanings born of religion, new meanings will be imposed on it. When religious transcendence is excluded, when the public square has been swept clean of deficit sectarianism, then the space is open to the Seven Demons aspiring to transcendent authority.

This is how it happened with Hitler and with Stalin. So, when we look at recent developments here as well as elsewhere, we see a resurgence of publicly potent religions. This means that we need to look for quite an unprecedented way of relating politics to religion. I doubt if people can force themselves into thinking religiously at one moment, and secularly at another. The old rigid, simplistic separation does not seem to be an adequate answer. The question is not whether religion and politics should mix, because inescapably they do, like it or not. The question is, rather, whether we can devise a forum for that and allow this interaction to be positive, so that we can refine rather than destroy liberal democracy.

KRISHEN KHANNA: I am the only artist around here. So I am in a minority and I do not really belong either to the philosophical world or the world of engineers, politicians or religious leaders. In a way, I am an outcast. Yet I think that my particular field of activity contains everything. It is wide open. I do not preach on art. I can only talk about art because it is the activity that I happen to be involved with most of my time, and I see analogies between it and public behaviour, and the prevailing external conditions. There are the theorists on art, who can talk about aesthetic theories; and there are the artists, those who actually 'do' art. The two are very different. This is analogous to the difference between religious and theological teaching and the actual practice of religion in our daily lives. There cannot be any art unless it is actually practised.

In the pursuit of art, the past disappears. It is not that one is ignorant of the past, but that the present is so important and so incumbent that one is aware only of what is right here. One cannot obtain solutions from a memory, from a past heritage. Nor does this pursuit direct itself to a pleasurable future, to what has been called the pursuit of happiness. I do not believe that the pursuit of art is the pursuit of happiness.

Certainly the activity of art, for instance the activity of painting, is not a happy activity, unless one goes into a semantic discussion on this. In fact, it arises out of a state of great personal agitation and discomfort. One is not always sure that what one is doing will

48

work out. When it does work out, there is a feeling that it is over and done with, and there is some sense of satisfaction that one has achieved something, a small part of what one had set out to do. Indeed, things happen which one did not even imagine could happen and therein lies the excitement of this particular activity. One is barely aware of what is going to happen in art. The next move is never premeditated.

I cannot plan out the next stroke because each stroke flows out of what I have just done. What art does, maybe selfishly, is to give me a very intense feeling of living from moment to moment and in that, I think, the ego—or our infantile narcissism as Sudhir Kakar described it—is forgotten for that period of time. There is a complete absorption with the materials that one is manipulating; at the same time one is completely unaware of one's separateness from those materials; one forgets that one is a manipulator. It is an action in process which continues to the end, whether there is an actual end to it or not, because painting today does not really have a beginning or end. Painting is a continuous process. It is never finished even if one painting is 'finished'. Each painting is complete and perfect in itself, yet each is open-ended and carries on into the next one. One could think of painting, the activity of art, as a kind of never-ending journey.

The danger is when painting becomes institutionalised, when formulae are made, when ready-made solutions are trotted out. I think this leads to sterility, to a kind of 'non-art'. A painting made under such circumstances may look very pleasing and beautiful, and it may be very nice to hang up in a drawing-room. But that is all it is—and the painter has been involved only in object-making, creating objects that fit readily into a consumer economy, objects that can be and are consumed. This is not art. On the contrary, art refuses its own consumption. It is an activity of the mind, of the spirit. It insists that painting be a completely uncharted arena in which things can happen.

When one of my paintings goes out into the world, it ceases to be mine. It belongs then to everybody. Certainly, everybody else does not love it as I do. But somewhere, some people might respond to it, and it then becomes an area of shared experience, of shared feelings. It becomes the passing on of a certain state of mind. And what more

49

can one expect from painting! Understanding a painting depends on how deeply you look at it, just as meaning in religion arises out of the perceptions we bring to bear on it. It is also dependent on the passion that both creator and viewer bring to bear on painting. Every person has a certain measure of understanding, a certain capacity to absorb things. Accordingly, a painting will mean less or more to each person. But painting is certainly not a hobby, nor pleasurable as such. It is very pleasurable, for example, to sit in the evening with a glass of whiskey and relax with friends. The activity of painting is nothing like that. It is an extremely difficult activity.

I think it is only in confronting this difficult situation that there is some sense of human endeavour or involvement, a sense of human intensity. I think that is what living is really all about. I do not think one can sit down and think of being compassionate. One is disposed towards certain situations which are one's responsibility and, if they are accepted as such, one just discharges them to the best of one's ability. That can be very difficult, of course. One has to handle the situation; it is an existential situation which has to be lived through. One either does it well or badly. One tries to do it well.

H.D. SHOURIE: I am tempted to claim one privilege, Your Holiness, that apparently I am the man here who has lived longer than any of you. I am now in the 80th year of my life and enjoying every minute of it.

Throughout this long life I have been dealing in my work with the nuts and bolts of living, dealing with practical problems. Somehow I feel there is much that one can contribute in the field of action in a practical way, and that, Your Holiness, has always been my endeavour. In my mind, moreover, the micro-level and the macro-level flow into each other. I believe that by acting at the micro-level in practical ways one also acts/realises oneself at the macro-level of religion and philosophy. What do I mean by 'acting at the micro-level'? Let me give an example. I remember receiving a letter from a person who described himself as a total cripple from the waist downwards, and had been completely bedridden for the past five years. I went to meet him. I thought to myself that I would like to help him, and I did help him. I found that he was eligible for a pension. He had been a government servant and had received a bullet wound in an accident in Lucknow.

Crippled by this wound, he was now lying there in Janakpuri. I took the matter up with the Chief Secretary of the UP Government and ultimately was able to get a pension for him.

Projecting from this micro-level, it has given me enormous satisfaction to have taken up, for instance, the question of family pension extension to the widows who were deprived of it, in the Supreme Court of India. Your Holiness, as a result of a case which I submitted before the Supreme Court, more than 100,000 widows are now entitled to pensions which they had not received for the past two decades or more. I have taken a large number of cases to the Supreme Court, in which over a million old people have been able to get pensions which they were deprived of on account of a rule laid down by the Government of India in 1979. I have also taken up a matter that concerns the entire country, which is the non-implementation of the Consumer Protection Act; only a few days ago the Chief Justice of India handed down certain orders to the States. To my mind practical action is of paramount importance, amid all the problems of religion, philosophy and politics. These actions, arising out of and expressing themselves in the everyday world of work and mundane human problems, become for me a way of transcendence, a means whereby I can experience and practise compassion.

I invite a reference to page 13 of the paper which was circulated as embodying the thoughts of Your Holiness. On this page you mention the defence expenditure being incurred by the countries of the world, the total being in the order of 1,000 billion dollars a year. I was listening to a talk yesterday by the famous scientist and astronomer, Dr. Carl Sagan. He said that the population increase in the developing countries far exceeds that of the developed countries. For a poor man, children are an insurance for an otherwise insecure old age. This population increase is threatening the environment, ecology and entire future of this planet. Sagan said that if about 300 billion dollars could be transferred by the developed countries to the developing countries, it would make them more literate, it would give them more drinking water, it would give them better health and sanitation—in other words, more security, more life options, and as a result, the population growth would reduce.

Your Holiness, you have status in the world, you are visible.

Your voice is heard. If you could think of something to arouse the consciousness of the developed world, focusing its attention primarily on giving away a part of its resources to the developing world, to be used for education, literacy, health, sanitation and a consequent slowing down of the rate of population growth, this would inevitably lead to better ecology, a better environment, and a quicker saving of the globe. That would be a very fruitful exercise to my mind.

I can only end by quoting a line from a Christian hymn: " Keep thy my feet. I do not ask to see the distant scene, one step enough for me." One step is enough for me. If I can help a beggar, that is enough for me.

LAKSHMI C. JAIN: Implicit in the question of Universal Responsibility is the larger concern of how to deal with the problem of survival. It is only when survival is assured that we can ask ourselves what the purpose of life is. And it is only when we ask ourselves the question about the purpose of life that the question of our determining what we do with our life, what responsibility we bear, comes up.

His Holiness has said that we usually have an architect to give us a blueprint; we construct according to that blueprint and something durable comes out of that. But no construction is possible, unless each single brick that goes into it is a worthy brick. So also for the human race, an important question remains as to how to make ourselves worthy. After all, we can only reform ourselves. Yet we concern ourselves with the attempt to reform our neighbours, which is why we have the haunting question Subhash Malik rightly asked: why is it that although we have been talking for 3,000 years, we have achieved nothing? There was an anguish in his words, that despite this eternal wisdom—that the only thing we can reform, if at all, is ourselves—we do nothing about it. But, in fact, unless we reform ourselves we shall not be able to answer the question of the very purpose of life, nor get anywhere near assuming what may be called Universal Responsibility.

The words Universal Responsibility usually refer to our relations with other people. But we have to be qualified for that. A nurse has to be qualified to look after other people. Even a rickshaw-puller has to have a fitness certificate before he can carry his passengers safely. To be qualified for Universal Responsibility implies a turning inwards. While we have pursued industrialisation and growth rates with commendable results, they only answer one dimension of life.

There is emphasis in our philosophy on karma yoga. But the question arises: what action is worthy of the words 'karma yoga'? Clearly there can be no absolute blueprint for action, because in each human situation what is important is the source of the action, the motivation from inside that implies action. However, the constituency for action is enormous, whether it is pure suffering, pure fellowship or love. The present is very transitory. Already the pre-lunch session belongs to the past. It is in my memory and my memory is enriched by that. I can also look forward, in the same vein, to the continuation of this happiness in the future. So while these can be described as past, present and future, an enrichment process follows if we seize the present and we are able to do the right action.

One more point I would like to touch on is with regard to *ahimsa*. One young lady expressed some confusion because the *Gita* exhorts us to fight and do our duty, yet we also speak of *ahimsa*. When Gandhiji himself, who is described as an apostle of *ahimsa*, went to Champaran to organise the first *satyagraha*, he asked all the farmers who were agitating to remain non-violent. Next morning he received a report that the police had gone to the various villages, whereupon all the men immediately fled. The police said: "It is your duty, your *dharma*, to defend your women-folk and children. You should have done that in a non-violent way, and if you did not have the courage, you should have adopted other means to defend them." The discourse of the *Gita* addresses itself to larger issues and that is why I was very happy that His Holiness himself asked the question about our notion of justice. Because if we are pursuing all these matters, if we are thinking about the survival of human civilisation minus the pursuit of justice, it cannot happen because justice is linked with truth.

We are bent upon disregarding Buddha, disregarding Gandhi and his heritage. We are bent upon pursuing the narrowest of interests. In such a situation it does not seem likely that 500 years from now we will still have an Indian civilisation. The Jaisalmer desert may survive and some plants may yet grow there, but what about the kind of desert that we are pursuing without any larger purpose in life, without any broader outlook? We find this society today on bended knees before the State, asking to be told what culture should be, what education should be, how widows are to be taken care of through pensions, and so on. If society has abdicated every single responsibility of its own, the use of the words Universal Responsibility in our context, at the moment, seems very remote.

SANJIT (BUNKER) ROY: Almost 25 years ago, soon after finishing college, I started living and working in a village in Ajmer District called Tilonia. At that time I had not read Marx. I had not read Gandhi. I had not read anyone who could have told me what the rural areas were going to be like. The village was a total area of darkness for me to which I went with an open mind. I just wanted to do something and I knew, after helping out in a small way during the terrible famine in Bihar in 1966-67, that I would be able to contribute something. I did not know what I could do but I had a vague idea in my head. There was no clear blueprint, just the will and the determination. It had to be simple so that one person could accomplish it. I remember that the motivation to do, to act, was very strong.

Now as I look back over the past two and a half decades, it's possible to see the whole experience from a distance and sum up my feelings. It's a personal journey back through time, based on an interaction with a vast cross-section of very ordinary people who are never heard—they are always seen as a target or a beneficiary but never consulted and given a hearing as human beings, people who can think and also come up with an idea worth trying; who have been through very trying and tense times. I'm referring to the sort of person that Mahatma Gandhi called 'the last man', who is exploited, suppressed and never treated fairly or justly by the better-off people of the village. It is still true today. They are by far the most easy to identify but the most difficult to reach.

So the strongest impression in my mind is that there are two Indias. There is the India of the cities—the filthy rich, the destroyers of the environment, the exploiters of the natural resources who have a criminal surplus of everything and the arrogance to think they can plan and decide for others. This India knows how to waste but does not know how to live; it knows its rights but has no idea of its duties; it is literate but not educated. It has emotions but no compassion; it knows how to take and grab out of sheer greed but doesn't know how to give gracefully and share; it knows how to abuse and exploit the law so that its lifestyle is not affected; and it would use all its power and money and even adopt criminal illegal means to ensure the poor remain poor.

It is the literate people such as these who do not want change. It is the literate in the village who do not have faith in their age-old institutions, who look down on the people of the village and see them as illiterate, backward and primitive. It is the doctor and nurse who are never to be found in the dispensary, while patients wait: the teacher who is missing while children patiently wait: the engineer who makes roads and bridges that never survive the monsoon. It is the literate policeman who breaks the law in the village; the co-operative inspector who embezzles funds; and the forest guard who cuts trees for contractors so that forests disappear.

These crimes are committed, please note, by the literate not the educated poor in the village. These last have tremendous faith in their own institutions, in their *panchayats*, in their indigenous knowledge and their wisdom, and they are totally mystified by the behaviour of the literate man. If this is what reading and writing leads to, then it's much better to stay away from schools and adult literacy classes.

The fact is that the educated have survived for so many centuries without literacy—villages have survived for hundreds of years without the engineer, the doctor, the teacher, the co-operative inspector and the policeman. Indigenous institutions made laws and observed them, and enforced discipline without interference from outside. Their judgment was respected. In the current destruction and devaluing of multi-caste community institutions, single caste-based institutions have become very important, and social ostracisation is still feared.

It appears India has given up trying to understand *bharat*, as evidenced by the absence of any sincere move to dialogue, to try to understand and respect the villagers' decisions, even if these don't agree with preconceived policies and projects designed in urban areas to meet their needs. In the absence of any serious effort to listen to them directly, without intermediaries and self-interested politicians, we see the tragedy of the same short-sighted projects which benefit a few and lead to duplication and a colossal wastage of funds.

In Tilonia I saw it as a double tragedy. The poor knew the answers to improving the situation, but no one was prepared to listen to what they had to say. The difference was that I listened to them and put it into practice, not immediately but over a period of time. I realised that it's important to make mistakes, to go through the process of learning and unlearning for oneself. But what is even more crucial is the ability to confess one has made a mistake, and start again, make corrections and changes halfway. One is not doing this alone but with the whole organisation. This requires humility, transparency and open-ness to share information and knowledge with other colleagues and discuss, endlessly, what gradually needs to be done. Most of all it requires flexibility to be able to change priorities, innovate, recruit new types of people, share the responsibility of success and failure. Underlying all these processes is the basic and inherent need to trust and treat with respect the opinions, ideas and suggestions of others, however high or low in the organisation the person may be.

In Tilonia we asked ourselves, how is it possible to do without the literate man? The engineer, doctor and teacher have an equivalent in the village. Can these people be replaced and made redundant? Can we show that it is possible? We took the problem of drinking water, a basic need. There are hand pumps everywhere, but for months on end hundreds of hand pumps around the country are out of order, because they are said to be dependent on the engineers to repair them. The government has said the hand pumps are government property and the communities cannot repair them themselves. But we asked ourselves, do we really need an engineer, a trained driller to install and repair and maintain the pumps? Do we need a man with a paper degree who has never touched a hand pump, and doesn't take water from a hand pump because he prefers to live in a city, to understand how important it is in a village to keep the pump running all the time?

So we took an illiterate cycle repairer and an electric pump motor re-winding repairer living in the village and trained them to take the hand pump apart, identify the parts that needed replacement and put it back together again. One month of training demystified the whole process. While the engineer was saying it was 21st-century technology and needed years of training in an engineering college to be competent to install and repair it, here was Tilonia simplifying it to the illiterate rural youth village level. The engineering fraternity in the Public Health Engineering Department in Rajasthan was scandalised and up in arms about it. Now, several years later, the 'barefoot mechanic' or hand-pump *mistri* is a familiar and accepted sight. Women are now being trained to repair their own hand pumps: the urban trained literate engineer has finally received a good education.

Then there is the problem of children never going to school. On average, 60 to 70 percent of the poorer children in a village cannot afford to go to school in the mornings because they are needed to graze cattle, look after sheep and goats and be a part of the economic activity of the family. The teacher has no time to run classes in the evenings because it cuts into the private tuition fees he or she charges to coach weak students in government schools to pass exams. It is a known fact that schools are run in the morning to be convenient for the teachers, not for the students.

What was Tilonia's answer to this problem? It was to start school at night for the drop-out kids, the shepherd boys and girls who would never have had an opportunity to go to school otherwise. It is run by an unemployed rural youth from the same village, who was trained in Tilonia how to run a rural primary night-school. This is very different. The teacher comes from the village; he is not formally trained in a college, but someone who was rejected by or who failed to qualify for any government job in the formal system. What the children are exposed to is how government systems function; the curriculum concentrates on the village institutions and how the post office, the bank, the police station and the co-operative work. One hundred and fifty such schools are operational today, mostly in villages where there were no schools before. The attendance of girls at these night-schools has also increased. It has angered the Teachers' Union that its monopoly has been broken and its members have to prove their worth in the eyes of the community. This scheme of using 'failed' rural youth to run night-schools has been accepted by the State Government and has been replicated all over the State in another form.

The development of the human being is everything. How we provide an environment for a 'non-person' to develop himself and become a thinking, responsible human being should be the goal. We should not be in a hurry, even if it takes years. It's a costly, risky and invisible investment that we must believe in as primary and crucial. It is non-negotiable.

The use and application of technology should be seen to be keeping this faith in mind all the time. Should we allow technology to control our lives? Should we be scared of it, or should we treat it with respect without being intimidated by it? How do we demystify the most sophisticated of technologies and use them to our benefit? For example, the conventional view is that solar energy is much too complicated and expensive to be introduced in the rural areas. It needs government, it needs highly-trained solar and electronic engineers, it needs a back-up support to repair and maintain it which is just not available in the rural areas. In short, it is madness to try generating electricity from the sun. There are other much more important needs to be met.

When someone tells me this, it's reason enough to try to explode this myth. From humble beginnings in 1986 up to 1994, I am pleased to tell you that Tilonia has baffled the technologists in the urban areas and left them fumbling. A fully solar electrified campus is operational today in Tilonia, running 500 lights, eight computers, a water-testing laboratory and a solar pump installed and maintained by rural youth from the village who have never studied beyond primary school. The head of the section is a village priest, who still looks after the temple in a nearby village. It's possibly the only centre of its kind in the country.

Rural youth, both illiterate and semi-literate, have been trained to install solar units for electricity in non-electrified villages from Ladakh in Jammu & Kashmir to Trichy in Tamil Nadu. Five hundred houses have been electrified in 25 villages in Ladakh located 10,000 to 15,000 ft. up in the Himalayas. Abdul Karim, the first Ladakhi to install solar units in 1989, is the master trainer who has installed over 300 units himself. He can barely sign his name; but the units he has installed still produce three hours of light each day.

The point being made is that India is responsible for perpetuating the myths that bharat is still suffering from today. The mystification of paper degrees required to develop the poor in bharat is a myth. The need to bring alien expertise from the urban to the rural areas is a myth. The need to over-plan and formulate projects and policies while sitting in Delhi is a myth. That illiterate people do not know how to think and plan for themselves is a myth. That we need such urban trained professional people in the village at all, who have no respect for the poor, is the most expensive myth.

Give the poor the space to develop themselves. Leave them alone so that they can develop their self-confidence at their own pace. These are not issues that can be tackled in one financial year. There is no doubt that the biggest threat to developing the poor is the literate man.

SISTER LUCIA PANIKULAM: In the morning I was distracted somehow. Perhaps I was looking forward to a discussion on action. I do agree with the speakers who have very clearly said what can be done within our own capacity, and I support such activities. One of the participants mentioned that Universal Responsibility must begin with us. There is no question of thinking first of a mass movement and of one's own contribution afterwards.

For us, coming from a hospital situation, there is a constant struggle to make people aware of the importance of compassion and love. If one individual is able to analyse man's illness, how is it that our people in India and abroad, people of God, cannot find remedies for the illnesses of society? I support the view that we as individuals can do a lot. For example, our hospital started several programmes for the underprivileged and the poor. We cannot be happy watching the situation, hoping that change will take place sometime. Today is the day that change has to happen. And His Holiness has said that if there is any time for happiness, this is the time. I believe this. I also believe that divine providence will give us the blueprint for bringing about a change in the wider society, through genuine service.

I feel very happy that at least a group of us have been able to meet today. We can now go back and do something about bringing change to our own environment. That is a big achievement.

ANOTHER SPEAKER: Throughout my public life I have been a believer in action. But I also know that action cannot be separated from thought. Therefore, I was deeply impressed when I heard Mr. Bunker Roy, and that is the reason why I am responding. Because I do believe that despite all the progress we have made, and despite all that Gandhiji taught us, we have neglected the very basis of our existence. We have lost the real meaning of education. The literates are really the uneducated. I am reminded of a couplet by the great poet-philosopher Iqbal:

Teri be-ilmi ne rakhli manavta ki laj,
Alam fazal baich rahen hai apna dharam iman.

(It is the uneducated who have treasured the meaning of
      humanity,
For the educated have compromised on basic human values.)

But now the question arises regarding the transformation about which Mr. Roy spoke. How do we inject that into the mind? What Your Holiness said about truth and justice has great significance because, generally, we all feel committed to our own point of view. We tend to convey our ideas to others in a manner which might suggest that ours is the only, or at least the correct, understanding.

More bitterness, conflict and confrontation have been created in that process than by any other means. But, in fact, it is not what is being communicated that causes these problems but how it is communicated. Gandhiji did not agree with people who say that truth is bitter. Truth is not truth if it is bitter. Rather, he believed that there is something wrong in our way of conveying the truth that makes it bitter. We need to remember that what is important is not 'the truth' but how to convey that truth so that this bitterness, this hostility, this conflict and this hatred are not allowed to perpetuate themselves.

SUNIL ROY: One of Gandhiji's disciples rushed up to him and said: "Gandhiji, Gandhiji, our wild life is disappearing!" Gandhiji chuckled and replied,"Yes, but it is increasing in our cities." I am an environmentalist and I would like to go back to what Bunker has said. The villages are of crucial importance, it is true, but more importantly our biggest wastage of resources has been in another area. We talk of resources, we talk about land, water, air, but we have neglected our richest and most valuable resource, our human resource. In order to reclaim the whole we have to go back to the people. The people have a certain basic wisdom. The fact that despite this they have elected a succession of somewhat, shall we say, less than satisfactory rulers, is another matter. The point is that they do have their own wisdom and we can go back to it. For instance, we discovered the *panchayats* and revitalised them. Our people have a certain common sense that is 10 times more important than literacy. Our people have the capacity to re-cast themselves.

If there is any area in which it is possible for the citizens of this country to question, if not to criticise, policies of the post-Independence period it is in this field of education. In that context, I feel we must recognise holism absolutely, in environmental terms. Essentially, holism is said to be the capacity in nature to make the whole greater than the sum of the parts. I believe that if we can mobilise the people of this country, the total would be much greater than the numbers, the resources, and the capacity of this country.

SANJAY SINHA: I am also speaking as someone whose work is involved essentially with bharat rather than India. I was a little concerned earlier in the day that people were taking the term 'universal' a little too seriously. The entire discussion seemed to be on a fairly universal plane, in a high-sounding macro-perspective and I found myself wondering at one point what I was doing here.

It may be that when one is involved in rural development one tends to see things very much in a micro-perspective, so I would like to say that I am glad that Bunker amongst others has brought up this issue. It seems to me that action is really what Universal Responsibility is all about; action to achieve certain human goals, and by human goals I mean that we need to be responsible to other human beings. When we look at the situation in this country, we can further say that this has to be in the context of poverty. What should our goals be when we try to take action in the context of eradicating poverty? What is important for the poor people of this country?

I would see the following factors as important: first, obviously, is the access to assets—which has otherwise been described as the means of production—which enables a family to generate sufficient income to meet its minimum needs. Then there is the problem that a large majority of people are unable to achieve a certain basic standard of living and to have a certain level of security in that. When we look at statistics concerning the conditions of the poor in this country, there is a lot of fluctuation in the GNP and in people moving around the poverty line. What the government figures do not measure is what happens in the following year or five years hence, when people go below the poverty line again, when calamities occur and so on.

I think economic security is perhaps the most important factor, because it has a bearing on the access to means of production, and on economic security and access to justice. And here again I am not talking about justice as an abstract concept. If we look at the pursuit of justice purely in legalistic terms, as the constitution of India or the laws of India defines it, we clearly recognise that the average poor people of bharat do not have access to that justice, because it is dispensed in an institutional framework. It is also dispensed incredibly slowly and it requires the person to have certain resources in the first place. So the poor of this country have no access to justice even in legal terms, and any action which can be taken to improve the access to that justice will in the end, I think, lead us closer to the goal of Universal Responsibility.

RAMACHANDRA GANDHI: It is wonderful to try to make His Holiness' influence available to activism in the modern world, but I would like this influence not to be exhausted by activism. I do not think we can achieve anything like Universal Responsibility without achieving something like a more universal self-image. Here at this deep level of thinking about who we are, I think the presence of His Holiness can be really useful in the modern world. Unless our species learns to respect orders of reality that are not really human, I see no hope for life on earth. Unless we are able first to respect that which is least like us, for example nothingness, emptiness, outer space, empty time, our collectivism and activism will only clutter outer space with the waste matter of our so-called civilisation, and abort the future.

Likewise, we need to alter our self-image so that we can love also that which is not living. We have to think of nature as more than just raw material, for that view may make it possible to satisfy all human needs but is the emergence of fascism of the human species as I see it. The deep self-image of the spiritual traditions of humanity must be made available to each human being here. Unless we are able to respect the reality of non-human life, we will go on slaughtering non-human living beings. That will make anything like Universal Responsibility impossible. Unless we are able to see the divine inspiration of every activity of life, unless we are able to make very revolutionary changes in consciousness—and His Holiness can be effective here—then ours will be an activism gone berserk in the service of the human species against the rest of the universe.

ANIMA BOSE: I would like to preface my statement by saying this is the first opportunity that I have received to present some of my thoughts on peace studies and peace education in our country's educational system of the day. I would like to support the comment that the literate have failed and the educated have not. It makes me wonder about the kind of education we have received, and why we have been keeping quiet about it all this time. I think a revolution should have begun a long time ago in the educational world in our country.

The second thing I would like to say is that our dimension of education is really an imitation of another system from another country. The kind of education that we had in ancient India had a spiritual dimension, as did our ancient literature, but it was also applicable to everyday life. Education had a different kind of dimension in those days. There was, for instance, the *guru-shishya* relationship. In our time, however, education has been distorted. Teachers and learners are no longer partners in education. Is it possible for us to give a new dimension to relating our educational system to the tragedies, distortions and lifestyle that we have created? In relation to violence, we need to heighten our perception of non-violence and of peace. Too often we imply that peace is simply 'the absence of war', that when one person is not actually killing another, that is non-violence. There is no thought, as Ramu has just now said, of a deeper philosophical understanding of these ideas. We do not go deeper into the ethics of the situation.

Therefore, may I say that it is time for us who are sitting here to emphasise that education is for life and living and, if this is so, then we should make peace education and peace studies part of the core-curricula, where both students and teachers have an in-depth understanding of what life is meant to be. Life is for living. The imperative of our time is that the transmission of these ideas be taken much more seriously, not just for the purposes of theoretical discussion but in a way that can be transmitted to the next generation and to contemporary youth.

I was deeply impressed by His Holiness' perception of dealing with the problems of today in a very contemporary sense. This emphasis on the contemporary problems in the here and now with a new insight is what is going to save us. We need to emphasise interdependence, a holistic attitude towards life. We need to keep away from fragmenting a person, or the subject we are teaching and learning. We need to add a sense of values. We need to be sensitive to moral and ethical values.

I also want to say that the change of attitude in the western countries, especially among the youth, is not accidental. It is the result of 30 years' worth of effort. Peace studies were started a number of years ago. Whether at the level of parent education or formal education, family or degree education, all education should be innovative. It should be based on the understanding that education does not stop with schooling, but that it is really for enhancing life and living *per se.*

64

SESSION FOUR

The Role of Media and Education
Chairperson: Ms. Mrinal Pande

RADHIKA HERZBERGER: Bunker Roy's distinction between bharat and India gives me a point to start my presentation. I happen to find myself in a position where bharat and India are face-to-face, in Rayalseema in Andhra Pradesh, 15 kilometres from the small town of Madanapalle. Rayalseema literally means 'field of stones'. Here there is a boarding school of 350 students, from different parts of the country. Some come from the Middle East also, the children of affluent parents who represent what Bunker Roy would call India. On the other hand there is bharat, for their neighbours are subsistence-farmers and shepherds who have lived there since the neolithic time and have worked out a way of life for themselves which has lasted for thousands of years. My problem is to educate both sections. That is the challenge that we have set ourselves and I think we belong to a time when the challenge is a real one. I do not think the two halves can go on the way they are going, because this will take away the resource base of *bharat* that has sustained life for thousands of years. I think that is inevitable under the impact of the new economic order. Life itself is becoming a commodity and the poor are losing their own resource base. I do not think we can just remain like this.

Two halves must make a whole, and it is in this connection that I would like to read something I have here: "In the course of a philosophical discourse, the 2nd century philosopher Nagarjuna invoked Buddhist law as the friend to all living beings, "Sarva satva bandhava", implying that royal responsibility extends beyond human beings to all living beings. Similarly, Ashoka's edicts declare that the king desires the welfare of all living beings. And the Buddha himself, according to an 18th century Tibetan text, preached his doctrine among the birds." The Foundation under whose aegis we are meeting today calls up resonances of the doctrines of the great teachers. The time has come when we human beings are going to restore the balance in nature that the human species in its exclusive preoccupation with human needs and greed has lost.

The doctrine of Universal Responsibility and the Foundation and its traditions prepare the way for this challenge that is already upon us. Measured against the background of this challenge, the survival of life, what is education? Can formal education become the foundation of a new education, can compassion become the foundation of a new education? This question should be posed at various levels: at the level of knowledge, of attitudes and, finally, at the deeper level of a wider insight on which our conception of human nature depends. The relationship between knowledge and values in education is extremely complex. One mode of learning instils knowledge and a command of technology, which produces power and access to privileged positions in society. This aspect of learning was promoted by the 3rd century philosopher Vatsayana who said that right knowledge is the means to *dharma, artha* and *kama.*

Unfortunately, our experience of a more complex society has shown that there is not necessarily a relationship between the increase of knowledge and the increase of *dharma* or good action. It is not the educated who have brought the world to its present state but the privileged—the economist, the engineer and the scientist, with their advanced degrees. However, as the ancients recognised, there is another mode of learning which brings liberation, dispels false opinions and changes attitudes. At the simplest level education ought to liberate us from narrow prejudices based on caste, class, religion and the stereotyped images which are ingrained in a civilisation like ours.

Both the humanities and the science of biology can teach values so that we as students have a less self-centered view of ourselves and our society. Darwin's Theory of Human Origin destroys old prejudices about race and caste, by teaching that human beings have a common descent on the one hand, and are connected with all other living beings, intrinsically woven into a relation with the other.

To give another example, it is important to contrast the

66

methodology of historians in a culture which thoroughly blurs this relationship between myth and history. The contrast is between historical propositions, which are confirmed on the basis of evidence, and mythology which has to be interpreted within the wider field of detachment and historical prejudices. The detachment is an ancient virtue and plays an important role in the context of education, by freeing students from narrowly defining themselves in terms of the mythologised past. This may also enable them to understand their present situation with greater clarity. We can give several other examples of how subjects in humanities and in the sciences can be slanted towards changing students' attitudes and making them more rational and humane and less prejudiced.

But my concern here today is with the problem at the deeper level. Can a modern education system be based on the foundation of compassion as understood by Nagarjuna? For the ancient philosopher the basis of compassion was founded on the twin virtues of faith and non-dualistic wisdom. A personal space, if he does not transgress *dharma* because of worldly craving, hatred, fear and delusion. A person has wisdom if he feels non-dualistically and has faith in human beings whose lives are given over to the satisfaction of our growing needs.

Both society and nature can maintain a harmony of opposites if we can step out of these divisions, silently and without effort. Such a stepping out is possible because their opposites have dissolved, and in turn leads to such dissolving. Such action may create a new culture, a better social order, a different world. Education based on compassion must of necessity be holistic. It has to relate to matters in the curriculum. It also has to address the issues of head as well as heart.

AMRIK SINGH: There is a school of thought which believes that the key to development is education and another school of thought which believes the opposite—we have had some evidence of the latter in Bunker's talk. One thing is clear: there can be no progress without education. But how one defines education is rather important. Literacy, I agree, is not education. But literacy is a tool towards a certain movement and that tool becomes useful when two things co-exist. One is the ability to read and write, which is a simple tool. The second, which is equally important, is personal freedom and a sense of liberation. Without that it does not work.

You see, we have to look upon literacy as an agent of liberation. Today our people not only live in poverty; they also live under social and economic oppression. If we think that by teaching them to read a few lines, a few pages, we are going to liberate them, this is a very partial view of education. Earlier, we were talking of action. No action in India today has any meaning unless it means liberation for the people and liberation, as I said, is social as well as economic. Where we have fumbled very badly for these four decades is that we have thought of literacy as something mechanical. We have handled that very badly, too, and not attended to the other things.

We must understand this also from the point of view that liberation implies so many things. Have we, for example, ever stopped to inquire whether poor, illiterate villagers are oppressed by the fact that our decisions are taken in a language with which they have nothing in common? I do not want to start a controversy here with regard to the language issue, but why should we overlook the fact that, unless we use the same language with which the person in a village lives and operates, we are creating a social barrier?

I wish to offer a comment in connection not with education but with the media. Maybe Mrinal would have something to say about this. This morning I referred to religion as an ideology. Related to this, the kind of communication or message that the media gives to the common man is rather a faulty one. I am not the first person to say that religion essentially unites and should unite; we are not arguing about the fundamentals of religion, but religion as ideology and there, I think, our media has failed us. The media is also sometimes overtaken by all kinds of urges but once again, I would like to draw a distinction between literate and educated. The educated would probably not go wrong whereas the merely literate can very easily go wrong.

MRINAL PANDE: I will start with what Radhika raised. Can *dharma*, not religion, be made the basis for education? And on this subject I would like to go back to what His Holiness said in the morning about compassion being the basis of the concept of *dharma*. This compassion, I think, has been given the best description in the *Mahabharata*, which is a saga of war and the absence of peace. When Yaksha asked Yudhishtra what the supreme religion is, Yudhishtra said: "The total lack of aggression, combined with compassion, is the true *dharma.*" I think we need this basis in order to have a viable educational system. Without this we will be breeding literate illiterates as Bunker just pointed out— people with no compassion, no vision, no sense of responsibility. Ultimately, these are what all learning is about, whether they are learned from the family, from the illiterate grandmother or in a highly respected institute of education. We are living in a fragmented society and our sensibilities are deeply fractured. Because of that we find this fractured sensibility is visible within the educational system also. Ninety percent of our students go to schools where they are taught in the vernacular medium, in one Indian language or the other. This is only incidentally related to remunerative occupation, which means that the children who have access to an English-medium education in this country have a better chance of success as it is defined by society today. I think this is where the basic flaw in our educational system lies.

I ask three questions: why has education been described as a great leveller, when it does not in fact reduce disadvantages? Why does our school system breed these disadvantages? This is where a sensitive child learns for the first time the difference between bharat and India. And it scars him or her for life. Unless this scar is healed, we cannot teach him or her to be responsible because (s)he has not known the system to be responsible towards himself or herself.

The third question is, why is it that our educational system today has become a vehicle through which a normal Indian child learns casteism and sexism? Again, when we analyse we find a lack of compassion for women and minority groups at the heart of the system; they are dealt with only in a marginal fashion. The central philosophy of our educational system defines success in a male mould and thereby subjects such as science, mathematics, computers and technology are stamped with a kind of maleness that leads them to become vehicles for success.

The key to this level of education again is English. Those who do not have this viable key are left behind and the ones who have the key find that there is a perfect caste system or hierarchy in operation. What I am trying to say is that it is a very heartless system in its operative form. It may be a beautiful system as it is defined. But as a one-time teacher and current worker in the profession of journalism, I find the operative form of education and the media to be rather cruel to the disadvantaged and to the backward. And this way, as Amrik pointed out, the media has not been very responsible, because quite frequently it pays to be irresponsible. Development-journalism in media circles today comes lowest in the hierarchy or the inner caste system. The aggressive young journalists who come to us as reporters do not want to cover education or developmental areas. They all want to cover political events; they want to go and interview politicians. This is first taught to them in the educational institutions and further strengthened in the institutes of media, where media-journalism is being taught.

The practical reality of their profession and the official hierarchy support the system further. If you are a Hindi, Bangla or Gujarati-language journalist, you can ring up the minister but you will only talk to his or her PA at best and they will tell you that they will call you and give you the time. If you are an English-language journalist, you will be connected straightway to the big boss. So there is a further hierarchy and wherever there is hierarchy there are oppression, exploitation and ultimately a lack of compassion because of the great push and thrust going on in the field to reach the top.

To my mind, if education is to become what education is all about, it must detoxify this area. It must detoxify both the media and the minds of the students and give them what Yudhishtra said to Yaksha. We must also remember that it was only to Yudhishtra that Ved Vyas gave the boon of *prati smriti*, the ability to recollect all that has happened: that is what memory is all about. The ability to remember everything can be given only to the person who can forgive all that is to be forgiven in that memory. I think we need to give the students this *smriti*. Then only can we begin to feel that we are taking the human soul in our hands and trying to create a kind of education which might one day lead mankind to think, or to start to think, in the correct way about Universal Responsibility.

SUHASINI MULAY: I am a film-maker by profession, and my interest in the whole concept of media and use of media is essentially as a person who works, if you will, at the cutting edge of the kind of deliberation we are having today. There has been great

70

concern voiced, which I share, about the lack of compassion in our society. Unfortunately, I really do not agree with His Holiness' rather generous assessment that human beings are intrinsically compassionate by nature. I am not sure. If we look at children playing, they are not compassionate. Compassion is something that we are taught, that we learn, and we learn it because we are taught that if we want to receive compassion, if we want to receive sympathy, if we want to be understood, we have to learn to understand the other. I think it is this process of re-education that we are really looking at, re-education in terms of understanding our responsibility—our responsibility to ourself has to be curtailed in favour of a responsibility towards something larger than ourself.

In the field of film and film production I repeatedly come across the fact that I am working with my own perceptions of what is required, as a city person who goes to the village. It may take me a good seven days even to evolve the images that I can use. My perception of what would be understood by a villager in India has nothing to do with what the villager understands as meaningful images. The villagers not only have a different manner of thinking; but they have a completely different ethic and aesthetics from those which I perceive as acceptable. I think if we are going to talk in any constructive manner about trying to promote the idea of Universal Responsibility, we have to start with a process of de-educating the 'leaders' who are to do this and re-learning what is really required at a much larger level than ourselves. In this regard, I think the whole discussion about religion is relevant—religion as ideology, as faith, different ideologies, Marxist and non-Marxist, 'good' or 'bad'.

I think the first step is to promote the notion of faith in humanity itself. I am not sure how this can be done. But one thing is certain: we have to address ourselves to a more active idea of what can be done to promote this faith and take an activist responsibility, rather than just thinking about it. The blueprint needs to be drawn up, and pretty soon.

NIRMAL VERMA: I am sorry if I strike a discordant note in this entire discussion. As a member of the Communist Party in the early '40s and the '50s, I realised the appalling capacity of man to deceive himself. When there were labour camps in the Soviet Union, there were torture chambers in Nazi-Germany. I do not think many people in India believed in these things and they all had their own axe to grind. Truth was not the most important thing. After 40 years of evidence, proof, documents and books, when Gorbachev said, "Well, here is a country which is coming to a collapse," he was not saying anything new. It is something which has been said all along by people but they were lonely voices.

Today, in the presence of His Holiness, I want to speak about Tibet. I speak with the same anguish as I used to speak years ago about Czechoslovakia, about the people of the Soviet Union. What surprises me is that we are discussing all kinds of things except for one—the suffering of the Tibetan people. Here we have a small neighbour, a neighbouring country which has such close affinity with India, in culture, civilisation, its past. Its people are suffering. Yet for all our claims about human rights and democratic freedom, the Indian Government remains silent for diplomatic and political reasons. What about the Indian intellectuals and Indian public opinion? There has been a total silence about what is happening in Tibet today. What has come from my friends, Tibetan monks, has been low-key, very polite. They have been very discreet because they know they have to take shelter in India and they cannot take part in political activity. The Dalai Lama has to go to America and Germany to seek the support he does not get from India. India ought to be the first country to lend support to a country which is suffering the same genocide as did the Jews in Germany, and as millions of people did in the Soviet Union. I wonder about this. I do not know what has happened to us. I know it is not a political problem.

George Orwell said an intellectual was one who articulated the truth. But what is truth? Are not truth and justice linked concretely with the people or with the destiny of the people, even in a small country where libraries are being burned?

Mr. Akbar spoke about *bhay* and *abhay*. Yet the party to which Mr. Akbar belongs is the first party which tried to frighten the Muslims into a minority. Vaclav Havel, the President of the Czech Republic, said that morality lies in linking thinking and speaking. If we cannot recapture that morality in our thinking and speaking, then we are failing in our task. His Holiness' silent response to his question about justice and truth indicates to us that we have to answer not in words but in terms of our practice.

M. VARADARAJAN: I think the whole point of the discussion hinges on the interpretation of the universality of responsibility. When we talk of this, do we mean that we are embarking on a programme of giving everything to everyone in the world, equipping them individually with morality and thereby endowing them with all the virtues—bravery, a sense of responsibility, honesty in thought, speech and action? I do not think that is really the intention right now, because we have to take the fundamental ideas and go on with the task of ensuring Universal Responsibility.

Very rightly His Holiness focused on the need for compassion in this regard. The Hindu scriptures are full of gods and goddesses who confer a variety of favours on human beings—wealth, knowledge, etc. But I think one characteristic which is common to all goddesses is the infinite capacity to bestow compassion as a blessing. In the beautiful *kriti* of Dikshitar's in *Raga Amritavarshini*, there is a reference to the *devi* as Karunyamritavarshini, one who bestows the bounties of her compassion, or *karunya*, in a ceaseless torrent. And *karunya* is something which cannot be postulated as pertaining to societies of the developing world alone, nor only of the developed world. We have to start from the individual. Unless the individual becomes an instrument, a tool of conveying the spirit of compassion, I do not think the spirit of compassion can envelop societies and worlds. We have to start with Man before we proceed to Mankind. If each man can do something to help his fellow human being, then ultimately mankind will be helped. It is not a task to be taken lightly and it has to be done by each individual.

Your Holiness, you have spoken about the humanism that exists in all religions. Dr. Rafiq Zakaria explained very eloquently about the humanism in Islam, about the spirit of compassion there. In Christianity also, the voice of the Messiah was that of compassion. The voice of the Buddha was that of mercy and compassion. The voice of Guru Nanak is that of humanism and compassion. But where has that compassion disappeared to? Where has the spirit of *ahimsa* disappeared to? When Gandhiji spoke of *Ram Rajya*, he also thought of it, if not in a religious context, in a legendary context—that *Ram Rajya* will ensure truth, honesty, social justice and so on. But when we speak of *Ram Rajya* today, it means something else. It implies those who are superior and those who are inferior, those in the majority and those in the minority. The time has come for us to direct our energies to the rediscovery of that spirit of compassion.

MRINAL PANDE: Our discussions indicate that basically man—and woman—are at the centre of everything. And nothing can succeed unless they are looked upon as the basis of all effort and all attempts to help each other. I am really glad that Nirmal brought out a vital point which had been worrying me as well, the issue of Tibet. In our school-books and our media there is a kind of embarrassed silence on the subject. Once I raised this question in a television discussion. It was not appreciated and portions of it were deleted. It is time we do not have to put up with this kind of unnecessary censorship.

Fortunately or unfortunately, I was in China when the Tiananmen Square incidents took place. The first question I asked all the students was: "Are you agitating only for your own freedom or are you also agitating for Tibetans?" None of them had thought of the Tibetans. I told my companions that this movement would not succeed because it was rooted in selfishness. It did not therefore have a sense of responsibility. As a result, I thought the students would be very easily crushed. Had any of the students shown an awareness of the wider context in their urge for freedom, I am sure they would have been able to overcome the forces that were crushing them.

CONCLUSION

H.H. THE DALAI LAMA: I would like to thank all of you who have taken great interest in the discussions we have had and have contributed your ideas. I very much enjoyed being with you today. I have learnt many things and developed many new ideas.

I consider education to be like an instrument. Whether that instrument is used in the proper way or in the wrong way depends entirely on the user. It is the same with our brain. Our intelligence is something like an instrument. Whether we use that instrument properly or not depends on our good heart.

The human brain is a unique human quality. But because human beings have often misused their intelligence, the human brain is at the same time one of the most terrible of creations, a source of great trouble. The guarantee for the proper use of human intelligence is a good heart. I believe this comes from a deep awareness of human nature in the context of a larger time-frame than our immediate future. All negative human activity and mistaken actions are due to a lack of awareness or ignorance of reality and truth. So in education, I think that teachers must look at both the training of the mind and of the heart. I think both are equally important. Perhaps cultivating a good heart is even more important, because whatever education one has gained can be put to good use on the basis of a good heart. On the other hand, those people with brilliant minds and vast knowledge but without good hearts create more restlessness in their minds because of misunderstood desires that cannot be fulfilled.

I have voiced my opinion over many years on the proper education of Tibetan children in this country. The education system in India is derived from western education techniques. It is questionable whether such a system is suitable for this country. There is no doubt that it is very important right from the beginning to stress the importance of becoming a good human being; being good is to be compassionate and committed to the truth.

Many speakers expressed their concern about India out of a realistic and genuine desire for action. But the meaning and implications of Universal Responsibility are much larger. When we talk of universality we mean at least the whole of this planet. Often when I am speaking about Universal Responsibility it follows that I am also concerned with problems not related to Tibet. The whole nation of Tibet is fast disappearing from this earth, and this is not just the question of poverty. Tibet is part of this planet. We will all suffer unless the planet as a whole moves in the right direction. So, too, in the case of India, the country will face problems unless the general atmosphere on the planet improves.

Of course, we have to deal with our own day-to-day problems. But at the same time it is very important to think of the larger context and to have a wider perspective. This might seem to have no relevance, but I think it is very important. This morning, I somewhat emotionally said that in ancient times there were many people in this country who could see beyond the boundaries of India. Today I think you are lacking this. Generally, unless something happens in India itself you do not take the lead except when you are compelled to respond.

India is very important geographically, and I think this country is one of the most important nations in the spiritual field, too, in the techniques of developing a good heart. For the future of humanity I think India should take a more active role, rather than just concentrating on its own problems. I feel that although India became politically independent in 1947, it does not behave truly independently in other fields. So I often tell some Indian friends that India still needs the spirit of the Independence Movement. At that time Indians were fearless, selfless and principle-minded people.

I apologise for my opinion if I am wrong. I have spent most of my life in this country. So in a way my mind is filled with Indian spirituality—and my body is filled with Indian food! We are descendants of this country historically and culturally, so I feel a deep concern about it. Politically, also, the southern neighbour becomes more important when our eastern neighbour becomes hostile towards us.

76

These are some of the ideas constantly in my mind. I really appreciate all ideas and opinions. In one way I am disappointed that many of you are concerned with your own immediate problems. Of course, at a practical level one needs to move step by step. First one must be involved in one's own circle. But when we are talking about an idea for the future, you must talk about something beyond India. Thank you very much.

WORKSHOP ON
UNIVERSAL RESPONSIBILITY
AND
EDUCATION

INDIA INTERNATIONAL CENTRE
November 10th 1992

INTRODUCTION

RAJIV MEHROTRA: The Foundation for Universal Responsibility was established by His Holiness as an affirmation of his commitment to move beyond his formal role as Buddhist monk and the political agenda of a free Tibet. The Foundation works towards catalysing Universal Responsibility bred of the insights and experience of the interdependence of all sentient beings, of man and his environment, and man and his fellow human beings.

The Foundation does not seek to cultivate exclusivity nor to promote any single individual or world view. It seeks to bring together, it seeks the building of bridges of co-operation and understanding. While our agenda is an evolving one, His Holiness feels that two possible areas of our work might be in the fields of education and the media.

Traditionally, values were inculcated and transmitted through systems of education that embodied formal religious instruction in *madrasas*, monasteries and *gurukuls*. The imperatives of contemporary secularism have meant that our education system tends to exclude the formal transmission of any values to our young. The Foundation believes the education system offers a vital context to cultivate values, with or without religion. It is seeking insights and strategies that it can use to make a useful contribution as it evolves its agenda. It seeks to learn from the collective wisdom of all of you.

Today's workshop on Education and Universal Responsibility was first conceived of by a small group of people who met in Dharamsala to discuss and evolve both larger strategies and possible specific initiatives that the Foundation might take in this vital area. The interest we have evoked is overwhelming. More people responded to our invitation than we had imagined, and even more sought to be here to share in this process of dialogue and discovery. The Foundation is grateful to you all. Yet it has also meant that the space in this conference room has been somewhat stretched. We have at the last minute relocated to this slightly larger conference room, with a diminished opportunity for interaction and intimacy; I apologise for this.

His Holiness has told us that he looks forward to listening to people rather than talking himself. And, in a way, His Holiness really has no need to talk. His life and his very presence are an eloquent testimony to the ideals of wisdom and compassion, of Universal Responsibility. We are grateful that he has given us his time by agreeing to be here throughout the day.

H.H. THE DALAI LAMA: I would like to welcome all the participants. I think some of you are familiar with my views about the problems which humanity is facing. I believe that, generally speaking, we receive quite a good education. I think we have both the ability and the means to solve our problems and improve our world. Despite this, humanity faces many problems, which actually are self-created. Clearly we lack something. I believe we lack the right motivation and a broad perspective. We suffer from short-sightedness. Nobody intentionally creates suffering, but sometimes we act in ways that have negative consequences, both for others as well as for ourselves.

I believe, therefore, that a sense of Universal Responsibility is very important for today's world. The need for this can be seen clearly when we consider the field of modern economic relations which go beyond national boundaries. Global relationships require a sense of global responsibility. A new challenge the world is facing is the problem of environmental degradation. No single nation, however powerful, can solve that problem. The reality is that we are dependent on one another, but we do not seem to understand this fact or its implications. So, quite simply, we cannot solve one problem independently unless we have the fullest awareness of our relationships—with other people, other beings, the relationship of the particular problem to other problems, to other aspects of our life, etc. That is the reality, but we try to evade it.

I believe this sense of Universal Responsibility is something very essential. It entails, I think, a deeper awareness of reality. This is not a question of morality or ethics, but rather a question of our own survival. Whether we are religious believers or not, whether we belong to this ideology or that, we are all human beings. We are part of humanity. Naturally, then, the future of humanity depends on us and we are responsible for it. Our access today to modern science and technology has increased our ability to affect the environment and each others' lives. This is another reason why this deeper awareness of reality is essential. And education is extremely important for that.

I feel it is important that education equips people not only to find methods and means to solve their own problems, but also inculcates in young people the right kind of motivation and responsibility. Education today seems to emphasise specialisation in a particular field or area. But it seems to me that such emphasis on specialisation, to the neglect of an equal emphasis on the relatedness of all fields of inquiry and all areas of human activity, can itself be a problem. The specialists with their study and their knowledge become so focused in that particular area that nothing else seems relevant to them. They become so specialised that their world view becomes smaller. I think a more holistic view, a wider perspective, would be more helpful.

I consider education to be an instrument. Whether that instrument is used rightly or wrongly depends on our basic human motivation, on the spirituality that informs our motives. When I say spirituality, it is not a 'religious' thing. It means simply to become warmhearted human beings, with a deeper awareness of the world at large. These are my beliefs and my thoughts.

I am very grateful that you have taken the time and the trouble to come here. I welcome your suggestions and advice. I want to learn from you. Thank you.

SESSION ONE

The Need
Chairperson: Dr. Kapila Vatsyayan

KAPILA VATSYAYAN: *Param Pavan* His Holiness, friends. I do not think that my role as moderator requires any introductory remarks for this session. Also, since time is limited and His Holiness wants us to open out to the larger, limitless time-frame within our beings, the briefer we are the better it will be for a discussion. Today we have identified, in language, the words Education and Universal Responsibility. This is an identification in terms of both the space and time of our own outer and inner contexts, which gives us some notion of what education is about.

At last year's workshop, His Holiness began by speaking of what he considered Universal Responsibility to be, and he identified *ahimsa* as not only the absence of violence but a positive action, therefore compassion. I want to recall this in the light of the motivational aspects and responsibility that His Holiness has spoken about. Therefore, there is a responsibility first towards oneself and then to others, and then to understand what is others' responsibility. His Holiness did not speak explicitly about the enemy that we are always fighting, the enemy within which is manifested as suffering. [But this was implied] and I speak about it now as his instrument.

In the discussion last year he gave us something which lived with me for the whole year, in terms of what constitutes bodhicitta and therefore the Bodhisattva. Then there were the questions of definitions of happiness and therefore of richness and poorness defined, whether in economic or other terms. There was a very important issue which he raised: how both violence and suffering are motivated by anger and jealousy. These are matters at the core of the educational process, not to mention the other two instruments of this *Mahabharata* inside, namely fear and desire.

I think it necessary to place this as a context to our discussions, before we fall into the well-grooved railway lines of our very limited and highly specialised formal education and, in fact, as a possible brake on that course. My plea to my distinguished participants here would be to let go of those lines: we are all masters, some great, some skilful, some fast, some slow, but if we let go of all that today we might have a really meaningful dialogue. May I now call upon Dr. S. Anandalakshmy to speak. I am not going to start introducing people and, as Rajiv has said, the shorter the presentation, the better, in the sense that it would allow for some dialogue in its real meaning of communication, rather than a presentation of our understanding of what constitutes the 'I'.

S. ANANDALAKSHMY: I have been asked to identify the need for such a discussion and to identify the problems in the education system as faced by an academic who teaches in a university. However, I have also taught in a school, with the constant memory of what I enjoyed the most as a student. So I think the first brief experience I shall cite will be one from my own experience as a school student, and then an insight from a school that I have been studying as an educationalist, and finally a comment on our surrender of a sense of the sacred in our educational system.

One of the most unforgettable experiences of my school days was when I was about nine years old, and I was being taken out to feel the first rain of the monsoon. Our teacher said, "Let us go and feel the rain." And he asked us to follow the leader when we went out. This was in Madras and we had access to the beach. So all of us ran out and there we were on the beach, following the leader, running and jumping. It seems a simple thing, but it was one of the most exciting educational experiences that I have retained throughout my life, the spirit of which I have tried to bring to my classes even if I was teaching postgraduate class in the University. There was a sense of experiencing directly, but also the discipline of following the leader, the joy of being together with others, the sharing of a sense of both one's own humanity and that of oneness with nature, of experiencing rain not as enemy but as something to be experienced fresh from the sky.

The second insight I had comes from a study that I am now doing on a rural school, Neel Bagh in Karnataka. It was a very unusual system; children of totally uneducated parents came into that system, and were able to become very interesting, lively human beings with good minds and cultivated interests. I am now doing a study of the children who came out of that school. One of the ex-pupils said: "More than anything else, we were treated with so much affection by the teacher. He really treated us as his own children." In her letter to me, she writes: "No one else has given me love so unreservedly. And that I remember the most."

The point I am making is that while we have to produce the best, while we have to value excellence and train students to work for that, it does not have the same impact if it is done in a cold and unemotional way. We all know that however good a teacher someone may be, it is not only brilliance which really brings us to him but his large humanity—some warmth that he communicates, some love that he is able to express. This was done at Neel Bagh by David Horsburgh; his qualities were captured in my interviews with his old students.

The third point I would like to make comes out of a study of classical music lessons in Madras. When I analysed it as a social scientist, when I tried to understand what the learning of music involved, I realised that one could not have classical music lessons without gaining a concept of the sacred. The composer I studied had gone on a pilgrimage in creating five songs. Each one represented the *pancha mahabhutas vayu, akasha, prithvi* and so on, and each became holistically combined with the philosophy of existence and relationships. It would have been impossible to be a music student in that situation without a concept of the sacred.

I realised straightaway that if there is a sort of cut-off point between modern and traditional education, it is that in modern education we seem to be giving up what is sacred in our pursuit of what is secular or profane—profane meaning beyond the temple, outside the temple. I have also been educated in the modern university system. We are forced to educate, to convey the deepest values, without ever mentioning anything sacred. Our sense of the sacred has to be kept implicit. In such a situation the teacher has to convey this sense of the sacred, this holistic relationship of human life and the life of the universe, without explicitly referring to any of these concepts, because 'modern' education has to meet the demands of 'secular' values. In order to do this, the teacher has to have both integrity and passion. To convey it at all, despite the system of education, is the real challenge.

ANANYA VAJPEYI: I am clearly in too educated and too well-informed company to state the obvious about the many limitations of the current system of education—be it the question of our syllabi, our language policy, or the failure of the examination system. Most people here are educationalists and teachers and I do not believe there is a need for me as a student to point out the fact that education in India is neither structured nor flexible enough to be successful in any of its aims.

Instead, I begin with a small quotation from Sanskrit which has helped me to clarify a lot of thoughts and which I would like to share with you: "Na mantra maksharam"—"There is no syllable which is not potentially a mantra." Similarly, there is no organic substance which does not have potential medicinal value. There is no human being who does not have some ability or talent. If there is a lack, it is of a person or a system or a process that can discover and activate this hidden potential in each being. And when I thought about it, it seemed to me that really education has just this function, to reveal the hidden facets of those students, helping them to emerge—and that is precisely where education today is failing.

There is one particular problem on which I would like to focus, which is that our textbooks give very short shrift to our spiritual and cultural heritage. We learn, for instance, the minimum number of facts possible, such as the names of major religious sites and monuments, and a list of festivals. The excuse given for this unimaginative treatment of what is perhaps the world's richest mine of cultural information is that, in a system open to all communities, nothing that has a remotely religious nature can be legitimately given emphasis. And the argument given, the so-called secular argument, is that it is better that our children know nothing than to know and to quarrel with each other. In this way, as I see it, the system institutionalises cultural ignorance, arising from the fear of handling India's cultural complexity, and from the inability to differentiate, as His Holiness has pointed out, between the religious and the spiritual. As a result we are losing out on all that has aesthetic, ecological and truly secular value in various cultural phenomena.

The educational machinery simply fails to communicate so much to us that has an organic connection with the indigenous pattern of life. For instance, most festivals are primarily related to the agricultural cycle and the coming and going of the seasons. But our misunderstanding of what is secular causes us to avoid dwelling on these relationships. All of this becomes then the submerged, untellable story of secular India. In one fell swoop we are distanced from the practical, functional, anthropological dimensions of various rituals and festivals, yet at the same time we become fanatical about what we imagine are their ideological implications. I assume that everyone will agree that the *Ram Janambhoomi* situation has come to pass because of the politicisation and commercialisation of religion. Take this a step further and we can put a lot of blame for that on the failure of the educational system to prepare students to combat this kind of blatant onslaught on their rationality by political and commercial forces.

As a developing nation, there is deprivation in the Indian context. We are a deprived nation. But the worst kind of deprivation is that which we are obviously inflicting on ourselves by denying our priceless heritage its rightful place in our school books and thereby in the minds of crores of young Indians. We are poor, anyway, but as far as I can see we are likely to remain poor despite all the economic aid in the world, because we are insisting on ensuring the spiritual and cultural poverty of the coming generation.

Finally, something small: when I spent three years in the Lady Shriram College for Women as an undergraduate, many students there realised that as our academic workload was increasing and our disciplines were becoming more complex, we were feeling more and more bewildered. We were unsure of our identity as Indians, as women and, worst of all, we were unwilling to act. Finally we decided to try and somehow relink ourselves to our tradition and our heritage. A small group of us would sit down and talk, attempting to evolve some basic simple rituals to make everyday college activities more fulfilling and meaningful. The attempt eventually resulted in communion at various levels. We wanted to remedy the gaps in our education,

89

to create some sort of fund or substance—I do not know what other word to use. To find a substance within us, from which we could draw sustenance. I hope that during this workshop—especially in the third session which is on religion in education—we can talk about this, because I know that people are in a position to translate ideas and strategies into concrete action.

CHATURVEDI BADRINATH: I am in complete agreement with what Ananya said about the present system of education. She was stating the profound truth when she said that the purpose of any education, formal or informal, religious or even what is called secular education, is somehow to return an individual to himself or herself and to enable him or her to see where (s)he is placed in the system of relationships which constitutes life. And she is absolutely right that this is what education has failed to do. But it is not so much that it has failed to do it by its very nature. Rather, it is because the current system of education never undertook to do any such thing. This system of education that we have developed was never designed to fulfil the purposes of true education. In India today we have a system of modern education. Since it was the creation and the result of the ideological battles that were fought in Europe, particularly after the Enlightenment, it set up reason against tradition, more so after the advent of science. It sought to replace tradition and its alleged ignorance and irrationality with the rational way of looking at the world and the rational way of gaining knowledge.

This conflict was then imported into India where, in fact, neither in the intellectual history of the country nor in its social history does this conflict have any meaning. It was not a part of our world view either. In India there were never irreconcilable polarities in our understanding of the nature of reality. So this type of education imports an area of conflict which certainly did not belong to us.

The second thing is that the traditional understanding of education is not in terms of definitions but in terms of *lakshana*, or attributes. One of the methods that was followed in Indian thought was not to ask for definitions but to ask for *lakshana*. To take one example, the question is not, "What is truth?" but, "What are the attributes of truth?" Or the question is not, "What is happiness?"

but, "What are the attributes of happiness?" In other words, what is a person who is devoted to truth like, in his or her relationship to himself or herself and in relationship to the `other'?

I think the question of responsibility is a part, then, of the unified way of thinking, in which all human attributes are interrelated. It is this interrelation which has to be understood by a growing mind and, as I said, that is placed in a system of relationships. I think we would have to go into the notion of Universal Responsibility in great detail; these brief discussions won't do. This requires a much deeper exploration, because we somehow assume that as soon as we use the phrase Universal Responsibility everybody understands what it means, and that it is a coherent idea.

Let us go back, again, to the traditional method of understanding, nowhere better expressed than in the *Mahabharata*. The *Mahabharata* explores the question of method in great detail. The method is important. And the method is that, for example, when a proposal is made that *ahimsa paramo dharma*, immediately several questions are raised about it and it is challenged. It is challenged by Arjuna; it is challenged by Dharmaavyadha, the hunter at whose hands an arrogant *brahmana*, Kaushika, is to be humbled and learn what *dharma* is. In other words, there is not a single concept in the history of Indian thought which is not open to question. But are these ideas purely cerebral, merely a moral ideal? Or do they constitute an inherent part of man's being? This question of responsibility is likewise very complex.

In the history of Buddhism, too, the idea of the Bodhisattva was not left at that. It generated immense debate. Unless we open up all ideas to debate and then relate them to education, and what that education has to be, the whole system will continue to operate as it does today. And today it is oppressive and untruthful; it has absolutely no sense of responsibility. It does not equip the young mind, and I share Ananya's anguish and her perception. One of the most fruitful parts of my career was my involvement at one stage with students, and so I understand exactly what Ananya was saying. This whole system has to be replaced, but by what? There I suggest we have to go into a very detailed discussion of what the traditional method of understanding life and relationships was. Unless we do that, I am afraid we would be talking with little purpose, without leading to any social transformation.

91

LOKESH CHANDRA: A very pertinent question has been raised by Ananya, in keeping with the significance of her name which means 'not to be duplicated by anyone'. The words 'universalism' and 'responsibility' are appalling. Both remind one of a theocratic approach. The idea of responsibility implies that I am my brother's keeper. It is the diminution of the brother.

Like trees, human beings need to be rooted. Without roots neither a tree nor a human being can grow, foliate or flower. If we kill the roots, how do we foliate or blossom? Yet our society conspires to render us rootless, alienated. Unwittingly we try to cut ourselves off from our roots, trying to find sustenance instead in technology. But technology can only be a means, it cannot sustain life.

The present decade is the child of a post-communist and a post-consumerist world. Secularism was an *enfant terrible* of communism. With the death of communism the concept of secularism can find no solid support. Secularism is the desiccation of values. The emerging world essentially has to be a world where spiritual values are given their due place. In the 1960s, the Chinese intellectuals called the Cultural Revolution the 'thousand weeds'. We have left those 'thousand weeds' behind and the ideologies of that period have suffered a natural death. Ideologies are passing elements and cannot survive for long. They result in regimentation. They are new theocracies. They dehumanise people and denude them of a sense of responsibility. They are not universalism. Instead of static ideologies and their imposition, what we need perhaps is an inter-flow of cultures, of ever-new ideas that make us pilgrims of the eternal evolution, both physical and spiritual.

The problem of perceptions is particularly acute in India. Our education is geared to the training of bureaucrats or of technologists, and not of humanists or of scientists. Science as a dedicated discipline looks minimal on the Indian intellectual horizon, and in our lives. No resident Indian scientist has received the Nobel Prize since Independence.

Why an escape from excellence? It is a result of our system of education which disowns excellence as central to human evolution. It is significant that we do not have a Ministry of Education, but only a department under the Ministry of Human Resources Development. We think of ourselves as human resources and not as human beings. How much more catastrophic has the problem to become before we resurrect the correct perspective? Hard-set attitudes have tended to become rigid emboxments rather than open spaces, static ideologies rather than flexible ideas. A Sanskrit verse says: "Kshane kshane yan navatam upaiti, tadeva rupam ramaniyatayah"—"Everything that is great, that is worth striving for, is subject to constant change."

The human mind finds its only efflorescence in spaces that constantly change. The Communist or Communistic framework had made it is impossible to conceive of universalism or of responsibility in the true sense, whether personal, collective or of the State. In the freedom from ideological constraints, we will have to look within to be able to understand the depths that lead us to ever newer heights.

This imparts a different complexion to the idea of responsibility, which ceases to be a case of being our brother's keeper but becomes more of an organic, flowing relationship between ourself and the world. There is no rigid boundary between the world outside and the world within. Each person is a microcosm of the universe. What is within is also outside, what is external is a reflection of the depth within. Besides being a microcosm, we have to become a micro-theos—a divinised human being. This does not mean that we take on the contradictions of religion. Every system and institution has its contradictions. We have to move beyond them to the essential, but dynamic and fluid core.

I would like to end with a quotation from the Japanese *Hokke Sammai* or *Meditation on the Lotus Sutra*. It says: "All sins are like frost and dew, and so the sun of Wisdom can disperse them." It is wisdom, then, that we seek. Even wisdom is in constant danger of being petrified into ideologies, so the wisdom we seek has to be constantly moving. Even the Absolute, the *shunya*, evolves into *parama shunya*. So the Absolute modifies and moves. It has to be dynamic, otherwise it stifles life. We cannot think of universalism or of responsibility, individual or collective, in a framework dominated by The State. Every creature of the world is for us book, picture and mirror. We have to see the beyond within.

SHARADA JAIN: Educational engagement, as I understand it, rests on an act of faith; a faith that every individual is important and every single person has the potential to contribute something to society which is of universal value. The problem is how to go beyond a situation of imbalance, in which a certain kind of domination prevents a large number of people from manifesting their potential. This problem is not something intrinsic to the human condition. We created it and so we need to remove it.

The complexity of the problem is felt when we actually get down to doing something about it. Intervening in any situation requires a serious choice about an entry point. We all realise that everything is interrelated in our social situation. Therefore whatever we do appears extremely trivial compared to the totality of the problem. The triviality of our effort is a dampening thought, and somewhere it cramps us, robs us of the initiative to act. At another level we also know that we must begin somewhere. The universality of the problem, the global character of responsibility has therefore to be seen within the context of the particularity of the need to do it; specifically, in small ways. In actualising an idea we have to begin somewhere, from one small entry point. And there is a third facet to this. There is no uniform prescription for action. We have to go about it just by doing it, and learning by doing.

I realise that the little experience I have acquired, in trying to reach the unreached in the rural areas where access to education is barely possible, can contribute in a small way by being shared. It can be seen to converge into a fuller and more wide-ranging perspective. Such a perspective plan places particular experiences within the universal context and gives some kind of momentum and reinforcement to our efforts. We discover something concrete that can be done.

I will relate a very brief story before I end. When I visited a school with a mix of children in a remote rural village in Rajasthan, I asked one of the children to introduce the others. The child said: "This is Mangi, this is Gopya, this is Kalu, and this is Gitabai Shah." In Rajasthan, addressing someone with the full name—Gitabai Shah—implies more respect. This one girl was addressed more respectfully than the other children. Thus, the essential hierarchy within the village was contained in a new institution, a village school. One task could be to ensure that this hierarchy would be eliminated, at least in the school. It would be one small step to reduce the artificially propped-up dominance.

SUGATHA KUMARI: I work with mental patients, people who are totally neglected, totally unwanted, people who are among the most unfortunate; and so when I think of Universal Responsibility, it is love and compassion that well up in my mind. We all understand the concepts of universality and responsibility. Universal Responsibility is not something alien to Indian thought. We are a nation of people who chant, "Aham Brahma Asmi"—"I am Brahman." This means that no being is essentially different from any other being. By virtue of this perception, no one should despise anyone; that would mean one despising oneself. It is this philosophy that the West tended to refine for us.

The West changed much of ancient India. The invasion was not merely an armed one but an invasion of consumer goods and ideas; an invasion also by a religion which considered other beliefs as heathen; by a language which considered other languages barbaric. Of course the West brought a lot of welcome changes to India, but it wrought havoc on our ancient system of thought and life. The western people told us that our religion was primitive and our gods false, and we believed them. We lost many precious things, including the spirit of the *gurukula* system of education, where the prince and the village boy sat together at the feet of the guru and studied *shastras*. We lost our *panchayat* system, which gave power to the villagers to redress their grievances by themselves, justly, quickly and efficiently. We lost our system of agriculture, our local seeds, our water harvesting and manuring methods; we forgot that we had harmless pesticides of our own. Our indigenous medicine was almost lost.

We boasted about our gains, but we forgot what precious things we lost. We became elite in the western sense of the term. But have we any right to go to the Indian village, to the simple villager who bows his head and says humbly, "I am illiterate, I only know that the cycle of birth and death rolls on and everyone is caught up in that web." What right have we to teach him our western concepts, when he has not forgotten all that is traditional, all that is Indian, all that is simple and pure? But we are trying to pollute him with an alien touch.

Progress for us has come to mean merely economic progress. This has resulted in divisions of various types. We, the progressive elite, are divided in the name of religion, class, caste, creed and colour, whereas the naive village folk are not. Educating the so-called elite for Universal Responsibility is, I think, far more difficult than educating the simple villager who instinctively has a universal view of life. It is modern education that is trying to make the simple emulate the elite, to their detriment. The best education for these people who are simple and un-corrupted consists in making them realise the value of their original view of life, in helping them return to nature, in assisting them to remember and regain the things they have lost. They were once at peace with themselves and in harmony with nature. If we 'de-school' them of the wrong things we taught them, they will once again imbibe the spirit of their ceremonies, rituals, customs, music and art forms that were the spontaneous, joyful expressions of their total life.

It is here that Mahatma Gandhi becomes relevant. He never considered isolated life as real living, simple literacy as real education. Carried away by western thought and methods, we gave our people a kind of life and education that estranged them from their surroundings and weaned them away from traditional culture. Character building, Gandhiji said, is the foundation of life; it should take first place in true education. Only a structure erected on that foundation will last. Again, Gandhiji wanted to impart education through village handicrafts, which is livelihood as well as education. If implemented sincerely, this would have started a silent social revolution with far-reaching consequences.

Gandhiji pleaded for global thinking and local acting, but his plea went unheeded. It is unfortunate that India has never realised the significance of Gandhiji's words. If India continues to fail Gandhiji, especially at this critical juncture in our history, I think we are lost. Return to Gandhiji, that is the only way. For what Gandhiji taught us was no personal tenet. It was the epitome of our ancient wisdom, wisdom enshrined in our Vedic texts and expounded by the ancient seers. It embodied the universal religion and philosophy, Hinduism and Buddhism enunciated. Unlike the dry concept of western universal duty, it stressed Universal Responsibility based on love and compassion.

KAPILA VATSYAYAN: Perhaps we now need to make the meaning of Universal Responsibility more precise. Often we understand it conceptually when we speak in global terms, but we do not know how to translate it into action. Therefore I think it is necessary to define the meaning of the words a little more precisely.

H.H. THE DALAI LAMA: In my own case, this idea comes from a Buddhist motivation. When I was in China, I learnt a little about Marxism and internationalism and their concern for the poor people, the less privileged people. I observed that the Chinese believe that there are no national boundaries where the poor are concerned. All workers are the same. I was very greatly attracted to this way of thinking. And then I thought about the situation prevailing in the world between different nations, rich and poor, the North and the South. Morally there is something wrong.

In reality this gap remains. Even in the developed nations we find the same kind of problem. Within one country there is a gap between rich and poor. There is a big gap in our own country. When I was once in a big hotel here, I saw through the glass windows poor people working in the heat, while we were in air-conditioned comfort. And at night they just slept on the pavement. We have become so used to these contradictions that we forget about them.

Then there are problems within religion. At this moment, in what was formerly Yugoslavia, people are killing one another, killing innocent people. If we ask each individual who is involved in this killing the question, "What is your aim, your goal?" nobody will have a clear answer except simply to say, "Killing one another." It is only a handful of so-called leaders, in their hunger for power and from selfish motives, deliberately instigating others. Sometimes this is done in the name of religion, such as in Bodh Gaya and Ayodhya in this country. Scientists are also responsible. They have many achievements to their credit. But then many of these achievements, like the atom bomb, create new problems, new threats, new fears.

Education is fundamentally the basis for development. Human beings by nature have brilliant brains. Education is the key that helps us to utilise that brain, that ability. But education doesn't always work that way. Take our own Tibetan community here. Those people who came from the farmland were on the whole very honest. There were a few cases of theft occasionally but generally they were quite honest. As they acquired more knowledge they become more clever, more cunning. When I visited the Lahaul-Spiti area, the local Indian administrators often told me that the more education the Tibetans received, the more their qualities of honesty and humility seemed to degenerate. These administrators would express their concern about this.

So too with politics. There is nothing wrong with politics in itself. We need to have a political life. Politics is but an instrument to solve certain problems faced by society. Many people today consider politics to be dirty, but it is not politics that is dirty. Some people who are involved in politics make politics dirty by their behaviour. Similarly, religion can also become dirty. Everything becomes dirty. Why? Each field, each profession is great. But something is missing and therefore these professions become destructive. They create more trouble instead of helping humanity. What is the cause of this?

Perhaps the most important factor that inhibits us is narrow-mindedness, selfishness and short-sightedness. Yet to have a sense of self, to look after one's self, is not wrong. Without a strong sense of self we cannot develop self-confidence, determination, will-power. But what sense of self is this? Buddhists think that Buddha is the highest being and that each individual, even an insect, has the potential to become 'Buddha', one of these highest beings. So the sense of self, or some kind of acquisitive feeling, is very positive when it helps us develop self-confidence, determination and will-power.

But there is another sense of self which is narrow-minded, that can manifest as extreme selfishness and lead to self-destruction. In order to eliminate that kind of negative selfishness we simply need to realise that a narrow selfishness is wrong. We just think about it; we don't try to transform or change it. We can change our mental attitude through meditation, the practice of analytical meditation. We have to realise that our own interest is very closely linked with the interests of others. So in reality the benefit, happiness and interest of others is our own.

In order to achieve a happier life myself, I have to take care of others' welfare. If others become happier, they will look after me. I will have more friends, who will be reliable friends. If I disregard the rights and concerns of others, I will feel lonely and I will suffer. That is the reality. So here we need some kind of sense of others' welfare and interest. We recognise that actually this is for our own benefit. We see this everywhere—at the level of society and family, and at the national and international levels. This sense of concern for others is the key factor in our own happiness and future success. Someone living in a village does not need to have an abstract sense of Universal Responsibility, but rather a sense of his or her responsibility to others, starting with the family.

As I mentioned earlier, we are interdependent at the level of the modern economy and the environment. We need our neighbours. India and Tibet are affected by Chinese behaviour and we need good relations with China. India and Pakistan need to have good relations with each other. That is the reality. We make a demarcation between East and West. In the economic field, for instance, we can say that the West produces disposable consumer goods, like plastic glasses and in our culture, in the East, we tend to reuse these glasses and preserve them for much longer, particularly if we are poor people.

A country develops and articulates two types of policies—domestic and foreign. One policy for the 'internal' situation, another for the 'external'. Why should this be so? Our neighbours are, after all, our brothers. But when they are thought of as foreigners, outsiders, external, our dealings with them begin to change and they begin to be articulated through military strength and defence systems. Whereas if we thought of these same people as members of our family, as our brothers, we would have no need of defence systems or military force. It is essential to be close to our neighbours in the economic field as well. How else do we develop that closeness but through the sense of Universal Responsibility?

Sometimes I am not very sure how to give an exact meaning for the sense of Universal Responsibility. But perhaps I can explain it this way: I believe that all human activity that is born out of good motivation becomes positive. A scientist with full knowledge and a sense of responsibility will only conduct experiments which will help humanity. The negative consequences of others are so great that (s)he will not carry out such experiments. A sense of responsibility is the basis of his or her decisions.

This also operates in religion. For instance, I am a Buddhist and Buddhism is the best in my opinion. It is the most effective system for me. But this does not mean that Buddhism is best for everyone. I cannot say Buddhism is the best for everyone if I am respecting others' rights and really feeling concern for them. Because for someone else, some other religion is the most effective and the best. Therefore, along with a sense of responsibility for others, I have to also develop concern for them. I have to realise that these are human beings just like myself, who have every right to be happy, who have every right to overcome suffering. For me Buddhism is sufficient and I have no need for another religion. But when I think beyond myself I see clearly that we need many different religions, and I respect these other religions although they may differ from mine.

Faith in God and the theory of a soul are incorrect views for Buddhists, because from the Buddhist point of view there is no creator, there is no *atma*. But since I respect others' welfare and well-being, this becomes secondary. Although it is my personal belief that Buddhism is most effective, my sense of responsibility to others and their beliefs allows me to accept other views also.

Similarly, if we look at the relationship between teacher and student, teachers should not think of their own salary or their own profession. Their real concern should be the welfare of their students. They are educating them for their growth and evolution. If they communicate this, if they show their genuine concern, the students will also appreciate them. I was a lazy student myself. But when my teacher taught with the right kind of mood, that lesson went deep down. If the teacher was harsh that day, the lesson would not be successful.

PREM KIRPAL: Your Holiness, I wish to offer a word of tribute to your ideal of Universal Responsibility, and I think the time is ripe for such a dream to be fulfilled. I recall the year of 1945 when I worked at India House in London, serving our students and scholars in Britain. Just across from India House was the street in which the Society of Friends functioned. Its publisher, Victor Gollancs, brought out a pamphlet entitled *Am I My Brother's Keeper?* We all read it in those times of idealism and euphoria, after the great destruction wrought by the War.

A few steps away from India House was the Society of Engineers, where the Allied Ministers of Education were meeting, trying to evolve a constitution for UNESCO, thinking of the ways and means of building defences of peace in the minds of men, and dreaming about the moral and intellectual solidarity of mankind. Now that was a time when the need for Universal Responsibility, which you have so eloquently explained, was felt. But unfortunately, these things remained dreams. We did not become our brothers' keepers. We became exploiters of each other, and we continue to exploit each other. UNESCO also foundered in its own problems, both financial and moral. But as a student of history I believe that humanity has tremendous guts and energy to survive. Throughout, whether in small communities or large nations, we human beings have survived. For Universal Responsibility we need a new consciousness. It is not mere survival that is sought. This is a time of danger, because man and nature are both in great peril and we have to ensure their survival. But we have to examine the kind of survival in which we raise ourselves to what you have quite rightly called the attainment of the Buddha nature of a new consciousness. I believe that must be the objective of the new education.

I would conclude by making two suggestions on the realistic level, and one thought for further vision. In reality, what do we need in education? Education serves three aspects of a human being. It must create a person, as you said, and make a person realise this potential. It must create a citizen who lives with other people and becomes a keeper of his fellow beings. And then it must create a worker, one who must be in the world of work. Now, unfortunately, our existing system of education creates only persons in the world of work. People receive education because they want to be engineers, they want to be doctors. Yesterday I was at a very good school in our city. The teachers took me to a number of exhibitions which the children had put up. All these exhibitions focused on things which could be learned, acquired by the brain, or processes which could be explained by science and technology. There was very little awareness of humanities and the moral aspects of man. We have to create a new balance in the system of education and pay more attention to the creation of a full and complete person—the person, the citizen and the worker combined—and to the realisation of Buddha nature in each person. This system of education must work to make people live happily and harmoniously with each other. We must be citizens of the world.

My second simple, realistic thought is that we should concern ourselves with the modalities in a different way. At present we leave education to schools. Yet there are only a few schools of any quality. Mostly schools are neglected, and there are not enough teachers. So we have to mobilise school, home and society together. Education will not produce any great results unless we can bring together the tremendous resources of the school, the home and society, and in this mobilisation bring in the teacher as the central figure, thus invoking a new character. I would call such a character a 'mentor'. A mentor could be a grandfather, a friend or anyone— but he will always be a special kind of teacher.

Lastly, how do we create a new consciousness? Education must help in bringing about a new consciousness, a rousing of the human spirit in which human beings should be aware of their responsibility. Our responsibility must be to humanity and the human spirit, and I believe that can be realised by a new kind of consciousness developed by our understanding of time, space and eternity. I think these three must be put together. Personally I believe we have to bring the spirit and messages of the great religions of the world into this educational system.

Once again, Your Holiness, I wish you all success. I am sure that with your inspiration and guidance we will realise Universal Responsibility in our country, bringing in our traditions to help and our dreams to inspire, so that together we can bring a new consciousness to our society.

HORACE JACOB: There is a tendency among the educated elite to blame our problems on the West or other nations, or to find fault with the system for our inabilities or our lack of desire to evolve. I am a scientist, a physicist. Even the scientist has realised the lack of spirituality in scientific training. Science and technological advancement without the intervention of the spiritual dimensions of mankind has led to greed, hatred and delusion. Without that little thing which is absent, we end up with a so-called model of man, and not the moral and spiritual model of man where *karunya, abhay* and all these qualities are built into human beings.

Your Holiness, I appreciate your desire for universal consciousness. I teach in a Christian institution, where we too are trying to inculcate in our students some of the spiritual values which have universal appeal with, of course, the background of the teaching of Jesus Christ. I just want to point out something which was very dear to Mahatma Gandhi, and that is the Sermon on the Mount. I pick up the last words from that, where Jesus says, "We are the salt of the earth." To my mind, these words point to your desire for Universal Responsibility.

Our education s, stem must be such that we restore this divinity. The present education system has reduced us to mere coal in the machine. It has not inculcated human values in our students. It is high time that instead of elaborate discussions and seminars, etc., we get down to business and start inculcating these values right from the primary level of education where we have very tender, impressionable human beings to deal with.

Dr. Prem Kirpal pointed out that he visited one school and saw very elaborate scientific models, but that the element of humanity was missing. This element of humanity can be brought out by a consciousness given to mankind by the religions of the world. Universalisation as well as unification of all the good points in all religions is also necessary.

G.P. TALWAR: There is a crisis in education which has been pointed out time and again in different forums, but little initiative has been taken to address this. I hope that this workshop will not only consider the views and the wisdom of the many who are collected here but will continue in the form of some sort of initiative, however modest, which could become an example. This is an issue about which I feel nothing much has been done.

I would also like to say that we should not view education as merely something that happens in schools, colleges and like institutions. A great role is played by the home, too, and by the parents. Neurophysiological research indicates that a great deal becomes ingrained in the very early years. In fact, the mould is cast before the child goes to school. Schools, no doubt, have a great role to play and our next session is going to bring out the role of the teachers, classroom and so forth in education. I am anxious to ensure that this early part of the formation of a human being is not overlooked.

Your Holiness, you have given some clarification of what is implied by Universal Responsibility: a sort of value system which does not only see self-interest. Like all animals, man has basic instincts, of self-preservation and self-aggrandisement by whatever means. Our modern education, centred primarily on career achievements, is dehumanising. The concerns for the collectivity, for the community, are being lost along with wider social values. In your introductory remarks there seems to be yet another message, going beyond merely ethical reasons. We are confronting a crisis today, as at no other time in our history, where Mother Earth is being assaulted. India has two percent of the land area of the world and 16 percent of its population. Actions taken today in India as well as in many other countries are accelerating this crisis. Many such problems do not recognise borders. I think some attention needs to be given to this dimension of the universal problems which we confront by virtue of the developments that have taken place. I do not know whether there is enough time to discuss these important issues in this forum.

S.K. AGRAWALA: Many speakers this morning touched on the topic of moral responsibility. We have also discussed what has been done by the Government and the Planning Commission and organisations of scholars. It is quite apparent that many very responsible people, from different walks of life, are expressing the need for a sense of spirituality, of moral responsibility, of Universal Responsibility, in education. We may call this component an inner consciousness or a looking within, and it is clear that the lack of it is deeply felt.

But how can this concept of Universal Responsibility be inculcated? How can we go about having that consciousness of cosmos? This is the big problem before everybody and it requires a lot of *sadhna*. There are many who have not been in the habit of practising this *sadhna*—for example, the teachers who have been concerned only with inculcating skills amongst their students, with the result that these aspects have not been emphasised.

My second point was raised by Dr. Prem Kirpal. There is the question of combining the education of the school, home and society. A system needs to be evolved to inculcate some kind of moral education, which will allow a sense of inner consciousness to develop and come together in all these three entities which influence the mind of the child—home, school and society. The discussions thus far have not shown how to do this, although in His

Holiness' talk this morning he made a suggestion that it could be done in a particular fashion.

One last point that I would like to make is that the one system which we know did impart such values was the *guru-shishya* association, where the teacher was able to impart these values by his own conduct and his close association with the students. But now we are so many in number and there are so many values. So many pupils are receiving education, none of this obtained under the guru-shishya system. How can we translate the advantages of that system, and the values it imparted, into the present context? This is a question for which I have no answer, but I am sure some suggestions will emerge in the next session.

FATHER P.M. GREGORIOS: First of all I must express my deep gratitude for this seminar and for the fact that the very first three speakers I heard—Anandalakshmy, Ananya and Badrinath—really hit the nail on the head. I simply want to highlight two points that they made which are likely to get lost in this discussion.

First, it is not the case that we designed a good education system and it failed, but that there is a failure in the design itself. Whether we look at the Radhakrishnan Report or the Kothari Commission Report, they are badly designed. They are designed to treat human beings as resources and education as an investment. Unless we take care of the problem of designing education, we are not going to go far.

The second thing is to see that education is about relationships and about experiencing reality. Whatever we discuss, whether it be valuable education, value systems or quality character building, all of these things belong to the areas of relationships and of experiencing reality creatively. I would say that Universal Responsibility has to be emphasised in four basic relationships: first, in relation to the social reality of other human beings. Secondly, in relation to the environmental reality of all essential and non-essential beings, mountains, rivers and so on. Thirdly, in relation to the reality of oneself. And fourthly, in relation to the transcendental reality of the whole.

We must arrange these four relationships in such a way that the child is able to see the hidden aspect of these things, as Ananya eloquently said. A child has to learn to be creative in order to be fully responsible, because we cannot be responsible towards social

105

reality without work. Work is a tool whereby we can be responsible to our fellow beings. That is the purpose of work. And if we put everything in that context, rather than seeing things in terms of investment, I think we 'might then arrive at a better education system.

My last point is a question to which I do not have the answer. Why should the State tell me how my child should be educated? Even in the Christian, Hindu or Muslim institutions, the curriculum and the basic examining system are determined by the State. Why should it be like that? It is considered that we cannot fit into the present society unless we go through that system. We should revolt against the State's dominating control, which wrongfully imposes a secular ideology upon us. It also imposes an ideology in the religious institutions. That is a problem.

SUBHASH MALIK: Let me say something contrary to what has already been said, and you will forgive me for that. What has been said is not workable at all. The intellect cannot take us anywhere. We have been hearing about the love and compassion you have all been discussing for the last 2,000 years. And as for the educational system that you have been talking about: I am a product of the same and so are you. We all say everything is so horrible. But unless we start from the idea that life is great—that even in our misery it is great—and unless His Holiness is talking about that state of being, I do not agree with his words. But there is something in his presence that you and I have been talking about. Now what is it?

And what is education about? It is about learning and communication and relating. It is about empowerment. None of these can be done through the intellect, however. Furthermore, I can neither empower another, nor can someone else belittle me. In a sense these processes exist purely at an inner level of choiceless existence. After all, when we look at a flower and feel very joyous, the flower has not said, "I am so beautiful; look at me and I am going to transform you." These are things which just happen, and that is the quality of learning and experiencing.

The intellect can only talk about some things. It talks about yesterdays and tomorrows, but living in the past or the future does not change things. Nor does change come if we keep on saying that nothing is going to change in the next 2,000 years. Please do not live in that hope. If you are joyous now, then life is already transformed. Whatever your age, do not go on condemning everything, thinking that nothing good is happening and nothing beautiful is happening. What happens when you listen to good music or see an artwork? They transform you into a joyous state straightaway. You do not have to say anything. Such an experience is silent. I have been protesting against what His Holiness says and yet, every time I see him, something happens. He makes me feel great and I experience no resentment, no malice, no regrets.

I would like you to contemplate this dimension, which has been expressed in various other ways. One person's joys and smiles spread. The 'normal' social structure is: we do, we have and therefore we will be. But in fact this has to be reversed: first we are, then we do, and lastly we have. In our society we have reversed the true order, and there is confirmation of this in contemporary physics, and in all that is going on. The causation is not from downwards up, it is from up downwards. The universe is already unified. Why do we feel separate? That is the question. And it can be answered only through some analysis which is not intellectual but a coming together of ourself, the time and the context. Then things happen. Things are already happening.

H.K. KAUL: I think one important issue is that of the impact on education of communication technology and the information revolution. Your Holiness gave a view of reaching out to the world through very holy and holistic ways, but on the other hand there is the impact of the materialistic world which is created by the communications revolution—television and the other types of media. I feel that the child is like a bud and it has to bloom to cross the psychological blocks at home and in society, and the political, religious, national and various other blocks—until finally the child reaches the universal stage. In this process, education has a great role to play at each and every level. Education should act as a filter, filtering information and knowledge and passing it on at each stage.

RAKSHA TALWAR: My view of education comes first as a student, secondly as a mother, thirdly as a teacher and now recently as a grandmother. That statement embodies my views on education and how it can be imparted efficiently. I think we all have to be examples of the kind of person described by the theory of karma, but that is missing. I have seen time and time again the anguish of my own students, of my children and even now of my little grandchildren. They are confused and pained by the people around them, the so-called teachers who do not practise what they preach. I think what Mr. Malik was saying about sensing things is important. This is a very primary instinct that we all have. It is probably the most valuable instrument, but we have forgotten it. The emphasis has to be on positive action.

H.H. THE DALAI LAMA: I don't think that an expression of concern for the problems of the world is to be seen only as a negative attitude because, you see, it basically springs from hope for betterment. From that hope springs some kind of effort to minimise problems and faults. The fact that there is concern about something clearly demonstrates that there is a need. We want to change these negative things. We can do this at a superficial level, which is often needed in the short term, and then we can go to a deeper level, the root of the problem. For the most part we are working at the conventional level. If we go deeper, the impulse for action stems from an understanding of what the Buddhist terms *shunyata*.

Techniques and Strategies for Transformation Through Education
Chairperson: Vibha Parthasarathi

VIBHA PARTHASARATHI: Just yesterday about this time, one of our old students who is now in his early 20s and at the National Institute of Design, was visiting our school. He said to me, "What is happening in the school that is real?" And the teacher in me got a jolt, because I got the message that 'real' things happen and 'unreal' things happen. I said, "What do you mean by 'real' things? Give me an example of something real that happened to you when you were in school." He had been with us for 14 years; without a second thought he replied that the real thing he remembered was Vasant Utsav. This was the six weeks of activity from Makar Sankranti onwards during the scheduled school time, sometime in the early 1980s, when the entire school collectively experienced the various facets of Vasant, the Spring season.

A year and a half of planning had gone into Vasant Utsav, in such a way that the children could feel the whole thing was spontaneous: the likes of Pandit Jasraj and Durga Prasad talked about how Vasant has affected classical music and dance; a Vaidyaraj talked about what this season means in terms of health, ill-health and nutritional requirements, and how Mother Nature helps in terms of the type of herbs that are available. There was a visit to the Ayurvedic Museum, as well as collecting various statements and *shlokas* by *charak* pertaining to herbs, health and seasons and then actual specimens of these herbs, some in dried form such as reeds or leaves, herbs, roots etc. The children did things like collecting *tesu* flowers and making dyes out of them. Thus they learned to do various things with *geru* and *mitti*, things which are traditionally done during this season. In the language classes they collected and read poems on colours and various aspects of Spring, and in movement workshops they experimented with the ways in which the body reacts to and sends messages about Vasant, imitating animals, showing their emotions and a whole lot of other things. In fact, there were 44 such activities in total for children from two to 18 years old. This young man labelled this experience as the 'real' thing which happened to him in his 14 years at the school.

When I asked him what was so real about it, he said, "The discoveries that I made about myself, about certain elements in our everyday living, about the seasons, the earth, certain traditions—because we went back to Kalidas and his description of Spring and back to the *Vedas* for *shlokas* about Vasant and we connected these with the environment. That's the holistic education that one is striving for today. All this made me discover an entirely new world, a world that I have valued so much since then, a world that has changed my consciousness."

Now this was done by teachers, basically as education, although we used a whole lot of resource people who could not physically be present in Delhi or among our own staff. And we had to stretch the formal aspect of the curriculum into an area of activities which involved experiences the teachers felt the children should have. We tried to fulfil at least some of the objectives we had delineated for this project, which was both formal and informal. It was during that time that I realised teachers are not just implementors of a certain curriculum, but also implementors of the aims of that curriculum, testing it in terms of the needs of the time and against the background of the relevant and specific contexts.

This is my introduction to what may be one of the aspects of our discussion, which would also pertain to the perhaps more important session earlier this morning. Because, as some people have said, this is the session which may open the door to some of the do-able things, and some of the things which are desirably do-able.

SATISH INAMDAR: I come from a village known as Thaguni near Bangalore, in the remote areas of Karnataka. I wish we had met under a Bodhi tree in the presence of His Holiness, with a few birds chirping around, and then asking questions about Universal Responsibility might not have been necessary at all.

Anyway, there we are. And I would like to begin from where we are, not go back to the history of man.

I wish to make a few observations and share my feelings with all of you, since we all are pilgrims on an unknown path. We need to respond to the given world situation with a sense of ability. It would be prudent to share our feelings, heart to heart, and understand each other instead of getting caught up in words, dogmas, opinions or conclusions. A dialogue is possible only when we can use words and understand their meanings, go beyond their limitations and communicate by translating them; otherwise we will only add to the fragmentation which already exists. When we consider techniques of transformation in education, the questions that come to my mind are, first, whose transformation and then, transformation by whom? And then regarding 'technique', which is a mechanical process, a repetition and imitation which can be applied and certain results obtained. There is no denying that it is useful in academia for the acquisition of information-based knowledge.

Today we are confronted with mass education—education designed to earn a livelihood, which means survival in a society comprised of ambition, pleasure and competitive pursuits. It expresses itself in the acquisition of wealth, power and social respectability. So survival no longer means understanding our own needs and living with sanity. Instead it means succumbing to all that the social world has created. This has left our educational system bereft not only of human values but even of simple human courtesies. We are rather unconscious of the relationship that man has to have with nature, animals and fellow beings. We are not concerned with others. We do not listen to others and we cannot see without prejudice. Modern technology has made the world physically small and accessible, but we have personally divided ourselves by religions, nationality, colour, economic conditions and what not. The divisions are endlesss and every man is against every other into the bargain. It is the tragic dilemma of man that he cannot be alone, yet he has not learnt the lesson of togetherness.

Now such a man wants a technique to transform another. Is it possible? Perhaps education is too dynamic a process for any mechanical activity. It constantly demands a fresh mind. We are well equipped with all the know-how our forefathers had and we have taken it to the furthermost limit with nuclear science. But, unfortunately, human values have remained dormant and the advent of science increases this gap. However, we are still desperately hoping that furtherance of some knowledge will also equip humanity in the psychological sphere. To me, as a student of life, transformation means human regeneration, a sense of affection, a sense of austerity *vis-à-vis* massive consumerism. But if we try to assert these ideas and use a missionary zeal to convert others, we only succeed in creating more and more reactions. Instead, can we with utter humility put the facts to others and make them understand and observe the state of affairs with a sense of freedom, without drawing any conclusions? Perhaps an open dialogue of like-minded persons can be extended to the educational institutions, but if we fail here we should not aspire to convert others anywhere else.

Can we create a conducive atmosphere in our schools, so that children have the freedom to develop a sense of observation, awareness and sensitivity? They have to feel free to learn, and they have to learn without prejudices which comes from the capacity to listen and to see. The question is not what to learn but how to learn. They can effect changes only from within, from their own violation of free will, finding out what they love to do. There has to be a faculty of discrimination and doubt. Hence authority, regimentation, reward and punishment create more problems and impediments. They have short-term results and are long-term disasters. We need to have not only mathematics, science and social studies in the academic curriculum but also the language of world communication.

Our children are not good at English today and are utterly bad at regional languages. In this way we have lost touch with our own society and keep importing pseudo-westernism, consumerism and so-called development. Equal importance should be given to music, arts and crafts, gardening, nature, study tours, home remedies for illnesses and health, mythology and folk tales. All these should not be treated as extra-curricular activities.

We need to generate a sense of togetherness, tolerance and ethics, morality and love for truth. This can be done through a dialogue and not through any dogmatic religion. The idea is to allow a child to feel free with a sense of order and responsibility. These dialogues demand a lot from teachers and parents alike. There has to be an acute intelligence and also deep affection for the child, allowing him to find out rather than pushing him into the academic market of examinations. Education is not only imprinting, but also finding a harmony within.

However corrupt the society may be, we cannot compartmentalise. We should not create ivory towers but an oasis of goodness. The child must see and appreciate the problems at first hand; and the same is true for the adults. The flowering of goodness in a child is simultaneously in the child, teacher and parents, and there is no place to move away from each other. If we raise such questions as, "Is it possible? Is it practicable? Is it worthwhile?" and if the feeling is there that "Only I know," then I fear we cannot make a beginning. We need to shift our basics in education from sheer livelihood to self-inquiry. It is the inquiring self which sets the right values for life. And the right values then point out the right information and knowledge. How can we have education that is holistic, that creates men and women who are not just academic but also have human hearts?

RAMLAL PARIKH: Firstly, I would say that the title of the dialogue today should have been slightly different. 'Education and Universal Responsibility' should have been 'Education *for* Universal Responsibility'. That is precisely where we have to change our strategies now. We have been thinking of education as one stream and the process of change as another parallel stream. There are these two parallel streams, but they never meet. We must say 'education for social transformation' and 'education for Universal Responsibility' as His Holiness has desired.

In terms of strategy, we must recognise two or three things. Firstly, that we have a formal education system of a certain shape, and we cannot ignore it, good or bad. There are 4.5 million students receiving higher education. Every year 1,000 more colleges are added to those that already exist. Our approach and strategies should be to inject all the value systems of Universal Responsibility into the educational system, which is vast enough, and once it picks up it can take it up from there rapidly. But it is very difficult to achieve a breakthrough. It may not appear very soon; however, there is no other alternative but to inject something into it, and then begin the process of change within the system.

The major change that we have to make is with regard to the kind of education being given, whether at the school or higher levels. The present system is dominated by a cognitive process of amassing information; knowledge is seen as this rather than as something linked to the development of skills and flowing out of experience. Yet it is not easy to effect change. Universities would resist change, for example. Academics— some of the best in the higher systems—are also change-resistant. In fact, everyone is afraid of change. And people are not so bothered about what will happen to society, to humanity, to mankind. Their concern is what will happen to their career. We now have a situation where students only select such information as helps them towards a career. They do not bother about information that helps them to work for society, the community and humanity. That is why it is important that the curriculum should include some components of experiential work.

As Gandhiji emphasised time and again, unless we integrate an element of community service into education, we can do nothing, because values are not imbibed by telling and teaching and putting them into the curriculum, but through work. If we want to develop compassion in our young men and women, we must make them work with the poor people. The day they start working with poor people in slums and villages, among landless labourers and orphans and in other deprived sectors of society, they will begin to imbibe certain values. The nation now requires community, humanity and, as His Holiness put it, independence of mind. We must now decide that nobody has the right to go and take formal education unless 20 percent of the curricular time in the education system is devoted to social service of some kind in the neighbourhood community—because while we are talking of global peace, we sometimes forget that charity begins at home.

If we do this, it is neither difficult nor a big change. Varadarajan is sitting here and the National Social Service which he helped to set up is a voluntary scheme which has given tremendously good results. Hundreds of students have changed their lives by undertaking to be part of the voluntary system of the National Social Service. 'Learning through service' must be the catchphrase. There

114

will be no change otherwise. I would like His Holiness to invite some Vice Chancellors for a session—about 20 or 30 at a time—and have a dialogue with them, to influence their thinking so that a meeting of hearts and minds may take place among them.

C.J. DASWANI: There is a disadvantage in speaking in the second session, because whatever one wanted to say has already been said. Therefore I will only put before you some of my experiences and expectations. I am saying nothing new. Let me start with what is happening in our educational system: in order to transform the structure, the *lakshanas* that Dr. Chaturvedi spoke about have to be identified. What are the lakshanas of the present system and how can we change them?

I often meet students who tell me they do not have to go to class. They pass the examination without going to class. Then I ask myself, what are classes for? Has the system made classroom interaction redundant? I also meet thousands of teachers, literally thousands, who do not go to their classes. They are happy when the students go on strikes. When I ask them why they are not concerned, they say, "We are doing our work." I ask them, "What is your work? Can you work without the students?" So this is the first *lakshana*. The system functions without teachers and students.

Although the system functions without teachers and students participating in it, both the system and society do not recognise any other form of education than the formal system. There are 16 crore children in our country in the age group six to 14, and only nine to 10 crore go to school. This means, of course, that six or seven crore children are out of school. And the system is not really concerned. It simply excludes all those who cannot join it and through that exclusion it disables rather than enables. It disables those who have no access to the system. In fact, the system does not really enable, but since the whole system is based on the fantasy that anyone who has been to school is enabled, we believe that the system enables. Moreover, the functionaries within the system, whether in schools, colleges or universities, bleed the system rather than feeding it. Ninety-seven percent of our educational outlay is spent on salaries. Only three percent is spent on other aspects.

Our system is not the survival of the intellectually fittest, but the survival of the most powerful and of the most resilient, those who can resist all kinds of pressures and still survive. So the powerful and the resilient survive. The process, as you all have wisely said, is superficial. It is restricted to information gathering, for recall at particular times through the examinations. The system and the process cripple the learner in his language, producing linguistic cripples. People do not control their own language, nor do they control the foreign language we have chosen. The system also cripples in another way, because the product of the educational system does not want to use his hands to work with. It cripples a person physically also.

Unfortunately, the parent has no part to play in the educational system in our country. Even a teacher, as a parent, does not say anything about the educational system. I have often offered to go to my children's school and talk to the teachers, but my children say, "Please do not come to our school. The teachers are not going to like it." So as a parent I must keep quiet. And society connives with the system, accepting our country's system without demur. These, then, are some of the attributes of the present educational system.

Nor does the system communicate values. Western education is not without values, but we have only imported the information, not the values. The product of the system, as a young participant said this morning, is unusable and devalued. Most of all, young people do not derive their moral and ethical values from the educational system. They derive these—good, bad and indifferent—from elsewhere. The teachers are not motivated; they feel no responsibility for the moral and ethical degradation around them.

I am convinced that human beings are basically good, basically benign. But the educational system corrupts the human child in various ways, from the day he or she enters school. And by the time the young person has left university, aged around 22 or 23, (s)he is thoroughly corrupted. Those who survive this influence of corruption are really hardy people. I agree with Dr. Malik that perhaps all of us have survived the corruption and that is why we are here. But we are too few.

How do we transform the system? I am certain that the system can be transformed. The transformation has to come from the realization that, at present, education is supplied: there is no real demand for it. It is supplied by the State and as a result an artificial demand is created. Worst of all, our education has no practical use in society. So demand and supply are artificially created and artificially met.

I agree with Dr. Prem Kirpal that, in order to transform the present system, we have to bring in the parent, as the decision-maker. Indian parents must see what the system is doing to their children, and must be made to ask for the transformation that is needed. We must bring in the parent, but also the child, of course, so that the entire enterprise may develop a concern for the child, the family and society. I would suggest that what we really want to do is to look at the possibility of creating a learning society rather than only worry about the supply of education. To create a learning society, perhaps we need not insist on the three R's to begin with. We could start with our oral tradition and slowly go on to the written tradition, maybe around the age of 10. I do not know if this would be feasible.

Somebody mentioned the traditional *gurukuls*. What has happened to the *gurukuls* is that there are *kulas* but no gurus. The students are *kulas*, but there are no gurus. Can gurus be created? I do not know! Perhaps this creating of gurus is the transformation that we must try and bring about.

H.H. THE DALAI LAMA: It is easy to see the problem, more difficult to know the causes, and even more difficult to find the remedy. Basically human nature is gentle. It is positive, although negative emotions are also part of the human mind. But these negative emotions are certainly not dominant. I consider human affection to be the dominant force in our mind. So human affection is the basis of survival and therefore there is hope.

What is the value of these good qualities? Here I would like to say something about spirituality. Usually people are under the impression that when we talk about love and compassion and forgiveness, these are 'religious' subjects, so that only believers need think about and practise these things. They are irrelevant to the non-believer. I think this is the basic confusion. These are individual imperatives whether we are believers or not.

There is no question of forgetting about compassion and

love. A human being has to have love for humanity. As long as we remain in human society, we need forgiveness, compassion and human affection. I have often mentioned that from the time of our birth, we may be free from any religion but we are not free from human affection. We receive milk from our mother from the first day of our life, and we would not survive without it. Therefore, in a way, religion is a sort of bonus. If we have it, very good. But even without it, we can manage and survive.

These good qualities like human affection are a question of survival. This is very clear. It is very important to make a distinction between religion and its specific beliefs and teachings, and the universal qualities of compassion and love. We need love. We need to be cared for. And in turn we need to love and care for others. Everybody loves himself. Even cunning people do something good for themselves.

VIBHA PARTHASARATHI: Thank you very much, Your Holiness. You have said we survive with affection. There is the belief that only the aggressive, the powerful or the resilient survive. What do you think?

H.H. THE DALAI LAMA: I think both are true. At one level we cannot survive without human affection, as I have said. That is a basic fact. Now in society, as it exists today, if we remain very humble we may suffer loss. Sometimes we need an aggressive attitude. At the socially created level, some individuals sustain or increase their temporary benefit through aggression. But I do not know if aggressiveness is the answer in the long run. And, also, aggressive behaviour can be of different types—perhaps we should call it 'forceful'? Such actions may be positive or negative. Positive aggressive actions arise out of sincere motivation, self-confidence and tireless effort. Sometimes that appears to be aggressive, but it is positive and there is no intention to disregard others' rights. I think some of Gandhi's actions were quite aggressive, but there was a strong positive motivation towards a correct goal.

SYED A.R. ZAIDI: Many lofty things have been said, but I would like to talk about the mechanism of education. It has been said that we reach the father through the mother, so I would like to devote myself to some house-keeping. There are some relatively successful universities in the world. I think we should look at their characteristics, and see if they can serve any purpose, including the lofty ones we have been talking about. The example I shall use is that of the university system in the United States, which I think is relatively successful. Of course, this system has been borrowed from 19th century England and Germany, which themselves can be traced back to the medieval universities, which go back to the period of the academy and that goes back to the period of the *ashram*. So we have here a certain continuity with the traditions that have been discussed.

The kind of education we want to talk about is a liberal arts education, 'liberal' meaning 'like a free man'—the type of education not for slaves but for free men. There are two characteristics of a liberal arts education today which I find significant: the emphasis on breadth and on initiative. These emphases are lacking in our system. We start specialising at the age of 16, and then we narrow this down still further at the university level to just two subjects, like physics and chemistry, or political science and something else. I would say that from the practical point of view this is not a good way to arrange things, far less from a more lofty perspective.

I think it would be impossible in the Indian context, because of our narrowness, to create liberal arts educated people. That is why, even though we have people with good minds and abilities, we do not have any great intellectuals. The aspect of initiative is also lacking. Again, because we have adopted the model of the University of London in the 19th century, we have geared everything to a terminal examination which is very sapping of initiative. I cannot get any work out of my students. I would like to ask them to write a five-page paper every week and discuss it, and in that way carry most of the burden. Because I cannot do that, I have no sanction over them. They would think me ridiculous if I asked them to do this kind of work.

What happens is that they just get filled up like buckets. They are not going to get an education, because we do not train our mind or discipline it until we try to do something ourself. And it really does not matter too much whether we are trying to do it in chemistry or philosophy. An educated person who could be useful in chemistry is not necessarily a person who has gone

119

through three years of memorising chemistry. When Watson went to join Francis Crick and Crick asked him, "Do you know anything about this particular subject matter?" Watson said he did not. They were discussing bacteria and viruses. Crick said: "It does not matter, because my idea is that any educated person can be brought right up to the cutting edge in any field in six weeks." So do we need a person who has memorised chemistry for three years, or do we need educated people who can enter any field? We do not need to specialise as much as we need a set of disciplines starting with initiative.

So the range of coverage for this educational system can be very broad. The prospectus of Stanford University mentions a 'distributional requirement', a course that ensures that one's education is broad enough. At Stanford every student is required to take this course. It is compulsory for the first two years of a four-year programme. Students are required to take one course from each of six areas. The first area is literature and fine arts, and the second is philosophy, social and religious thought. So they get a fairly good exposure. We can also see from this that religious instruction is going on in a very secular state, and not only at a private university like Stanford. There are departments of religious study everywhere. The third area is human development, behaviour and language; the fourth, social processes and institutions. The fifth area is natural sciences, and the sixth is technology and applied science.

In addition to that, they take three courses in western civilisation for a whole year, and they also have to take a foreign language. This is just in the first year or two. Thereafter they start specialising and declare their major field of study. They cannot devote more than one third of their time to any one department. This is to prevent intellectual parochialism. Their orientation is exactly the opposite of ours, which is precisely such an intellectual parochialism. We could very well adapt a model like this to our own needs and purposes, because it has a broad range of options. Under such a system, the university recognises itself as being responsible for the whole range of human knowledge; even if it must also apologise for the fact that it cannot do this, at least it recognises that it has obligations.

Just see what can be done at a place like Stanford and what

cannot be done here. I learned some years ago that the greatest authority on *Atharva Veda* was a man living in Delhi, surviving on the charity of his nephew. There is no way that the Indian university system can make room for a person like that. But even in the smallest college in the US, that person can be nurtured—because they have many courses, and they would simply offer this particular course. *Atharva Veda* is the most magical of the *Vedas*. We think that this is a collection of superstitions. But quantum physics has now revealed to us the craziness of the world, and people whose minds are open—as is the case with most physicists—might be intrigued to combine a study of *Atharva Veda* with physics, or with Sanskrit, Chinese studies, various systems of medicine, just about anything. In another system the student is free to make such interconnections.

It is ridiculous to talk of moral education, given our specialisation. There was a discussion five years ago on the need for moral education. One person from the Ministry of Education made a statement that the Ministry was in favour of this, and also thought that moral education should account for at least 100 marks out of 800! The Stanford curriculum has an emphasis on western civilisation. I would like a college in India or in South Asia to have something on world civilisation, because the world is really our home. I am disappointed with the nostalgia of people who simply want to restrict themselves to very small areas within the boundaries of present-day India. I think the aborigines of Australia have a great deal to teach everybody, for example, as have the pygmies of the Congo. It is not only the so-called 'higher civilisations' which are our inheritance.

Another point: since the university system starts with orientation to the sacred, a man like Pythagoras was a great *rishi*. He was somebody whose vision included all the realism of science and mathematics. He was not developing theories in the modern sense, nor is the whole of early Greek culture the development of theories as we know them. What Greek culture developed was theoria, from which our theories come. Theoria meditation, if translated into English, means something akin to 'temptation'. It means access to Theos, to God, and it is through theoria that the basic truths of mathematics and of cosmology

121

were first apprehended. I am not saying that they cannot be apprehended without theoria. But I would like to see a system where theoria is also made at least part of the curriculum, because I feel that we are in a very exciting period where, say, the cosmology that astrophysics is talking about is conversing with mythological cosmology, which is grounded in the theoria. And I think nobody can tell us more about this than people in India, except of course the Tibetans.

KIRAN SETH: I want to start with something Dr. Zaidi has just pointed out, something about the system in the US and something about the Indian system. I think there are some limitations in the western system, including at Stanford University where I was also a student. I would like to suggest that there are four stages in education: the imitative, suggestive, creative and finally the meditative. In the meditative stage, it remains no more an education but a direct expression of the soul, and this is its final aim. While the US system definitely reaches the third stage—the stage of the highest creativity—it falls short of that which I believe can be provided by people like His Holiness the Dalai Lama.

All this derives from an analogy given by the Sufi mystic Hazrat Inayat Khan Sahib. He described the four stages of the development of art as the imitative stage, suggestive stage, creative stage and the last stage which can only be developed through meditation, because it comes like a miracle. It is no longer art but a direct expression of the soul.

There is a very famous professor at Stanford University, David Siegmund. He is one of the best-known figures in the area of probability theory. I studied with him and learned a great deal from this master. But somehow, when he asked me to do a Ph.D under him, I couldn't accept this. While I respected him greatly, I did not want to become like him. When I look at this in retrospect, I feel that the reason for this was a fear of stopping at the third stage. Indian education today is unfortunately barely in stage two. In the past few years I have been travelling all over the country, visiting colleges and schools in about 100 cities; and I am shocked at the current state of education.

To give one or two glaring examples: I had been invited to deliver a lecture at the Holkar College in Indore and the Principal, with whom I was talking, was very apologetic that there were not enough students attending it. He explained that the vacation had finished a little early and the students had had another vacation about 14 days later; inbetween, many students had taken what is called GT or General Tadi and so they were not attending classes. I wondered why, in a prestigious college like Holkar, the students did not want to attend classes. Another example is that of a girl studying in a Gujarat college. She told me that in the previous year they had had classes for three days a week only. She said, "We used to come to college in the mornings, present ourselves to the teachers and then go for professional courses like NIIT, Apple, etc." It appears that professional and information-based courses have taken over.

Engineering, medicine, business administration and the administrative services are attracting the brightest of our students these days. Areas like philosophy, literature, pure sciences, classical music and classical languages are seldom chosen by the bright students.

Because of this, people are increasingly unable to grasp the subtle and the abstract. Now what can we do in such a situation? We cannot change the attitude of parents. We cannot even change the formal system. There are big ministries at work which are very difficult to move. So the best way is to try outside the classroom. Some intervention has to be made to jolt the system out of the spiral in which it has been caught. This can be done only by some very powerful inspirational and abstract input into the education system. I think people like His Holiness, as well as writers, artists, philosophers and scholars should be invited to schools and colleges. All people, things and ideas that provide an inspiring input into our lives should be taken to as many schools and colleges as possible, to effect the change. Hopefully, children experiencing such interactions will, when they become parents and teachers, provide a better home ambience and a richer education to their own children.

VINOD RAINA: As a drop-out from the Brahminical culture of university study, and as an activist in education and the environment, what I have to say might be rough, ready and pragmatic, rather than a profound intellectual prescription. I ask to be excused for that. With regard to transformation from outside the classroom, I think one of the things to note is that when we talk of 'education' what comes to our mind is 'school' and 'colleges'—in other words, institutionalised education. This is really a sad thought because it denies that education can happen in any other form. Moreover, it has a profound effect on education as we know it in schools and in society itself.

On the one hand, such thinking legitimises whatever is done in schools. On the other, it delegitimises social processes. Therefore, I am doubtful when we have suggestions like involving parents in school education. Once parents are brought in, it is assumed that they must conform to what is called 'school education'. Only then can the PTA be relevant. But a grandmother's story or a farmer's practice of agriculture is not going to be part of that process. And if they are not going to be part of that process, I think we cannot transform education from the outside. The only way to do it is to accept that the right processes are those which the child holistically experiences. These are the experiences which education should try to build upon, rather than subverting them by fragmentation, compartmentalising them into science, social science, moral education, value education and so on. Such categories are very atomistic; they are technological and reductionist.

I do not totally subscribe to your views. In my own experience, many of us hope that we can make things easy. We do not have to weep about how bad things are. What we need to do is to say how we can change them. We can prescribe that whatever happens as a classroom activity must also be related to, and not alienated from, the lives of the children. I am talking of my work experiences in the rural areas of Madhya Pradesh, in the face of extremely harsh social realities—feudalism, casteism, a general bias, anti-tribalism and so on. But something can be done. We need to see that nature is the laboratory for learning science. We need to see that the village is the laboratory for understanding society. We need not say that this is all we need to learn, but build on from there to things which are outside our experience. If we do this, we find that bridging school and society becomes a natural process.

We know that education is no longer considered a banking system, in which pieces of information must be put out in order to bring in a bit of interest at the age of 21, at which point the child is called a developed adult. It need not be that. It needs to be a process of analysis and synthesis. Children are not to be told what morals are; morals are to be part of that process. Children are not to be told what compassion is, because compassion is part of that learning process. And it is do-able. While we are doing it, we can fulfil the modern needs of learning science and technology, too. It is not as if science and technology are opposed to the learning of these modern notions. There is nothing intrinsically good or bad in tradition. But what is good in tradition and what is good in modern learning can be synthesised in the process of education. If we do it, we will find that a farmer, an artisan, a landless labourer, a mother, a grandmother, all have something to contribute to the totality of that education. We will free the teacher from the tyranny of our belief that (s)he is the only person who can teach.

We know that these things can be done easily in advanced, developed countries. What I would like to submit is that perhaps it is in the so-called impoverished areas of the world that it is possible to do this better than in the so-called developed areas, where the external influences on achieving this are far worse. The external transformation of education and, therefore, a consequent change in society, do not mean revolutionary re-schooling or a total dis-jointing of things. We must first, particularly at the school level, accept that diversity and plurality are the basis of education. Plurality includes languages and the environment. Diversity in-cludes all kinds of social diversity. These must be the basis for education, and be accepted as such.

If we use school as a homogenising agent, with a curriculum that everyone takes from class one onwards, we are starting from the wrong premise. But if we allow education to proceed in diver-sity and plurality, compassion is naturally built into it. I think we can go to a university which creates an alliance between diversi-ties, rather than to the homogenising system of the United States of America, which says Universal Responsibility is America's re-sponsibility. We are thinking instead of diversities and pluralities which ally to create a Universal Responsibility. I think that is precisely what education needs, and it can be done.

The Place of Religion in Education
Chairperson: Father Paul Mar Gregorios

FR. P.M. GREGORIOS: I am grateful for the privilege of participating in this seminar and especially for chairing this session, the topic of which is 'The Place of Religion in Education'. Both these words 'religion' and 'education' have been given a new meaning by our civilisation, which they did not have before the 18th century. In that century a great German philosopher, Moses Medelson, wrote an essay in which he said that education, culture and enlightenment were three new words in the German language. These words were the products of the European Enlightenment. The idea of education was centred in the idea of enlightenment. When we train our reasoning mind to be totally free from all the fetters of tradition and external authority, we become free, autonomous human adults.

Moses Medelson's essay says that it is dangerous to give education to everybody. It should be given only to the propertied class, because only this class can be truly autonomous, truly independent of the people, whereas the working-class man cannot be independent. He is always dependent on the employer and wages, so he should not be given too much education. Education is only for the propertied class and for the professional class, but with a distinction: a tutor living in the master's house and eating from his table should not be over-educated, because he is dependent on the master's table. He is not autonomous and unable to be genuinely free. That was the concept of education in the 18th century.

Religion, also, did not mean what it means now. What is the word for religion in our language? We have great difficulty in trying to find a meaning. Some people say the word for religion is *dharma*, others say *pradhaya*, still others say *matha*. But none of these things mean religion in the sense we use the word now. And in the English, German or French languages, there was no word for religion in the generic sense. The word religion had a very specific meaning, referring to those who were bound by a monastic role. Those who lived in a monastery were called religious, those who did not were secular. It was a very neat distinction and it had nothing to do with what we call religion today.

Then the Enlightenment decided to do three things to religion. The first was to banish it from the public realm, including the State, which resulted in the separation of church and State. Secondly, religion was made an individual matter, a matter of personal choice. Thirdly, religion was marginalised as of secondary importance, not to be used in education, medicine or any of the important things that human beings are concerned with; these had to be based on purely secular lines. So this whole business of religion underwent a transformation. But before that, I submit to you, religion and education were one and the same thing, an all-encompassing way of life with a certain attitude towards reality which governed all that a person did.

Neither education nor religion were compartments of life. They were the whole life. And even in our own tradition, here we spoke of *brahmacharya*, the period before *grahastya*, and with the meaning of 'moving in the Brahman'. This is both religious and educational. The separation of religion and education into two compartments is the creation of the European Enlightenment and the secular tradition, which we have inherited.

The second point I wish to make is based on an article I read which revealed how Sufis listen to sound. Not the sounds that go on around us, but the one single sound that pervades all reality, that is the foundation of reality. In order to listen to that single sound we have to shut out the other sounds which are constantly impinging upon us. The same is true of light. There are so many light images coming to us. But there is another light which is the true light, the foundation of all beings. And when we are able to listen to that sound and see that light, we have a totally different attitude towards sound and light and everything in this life changes. Our relationship with other human beings, our relationship with things, animals, with everything changes.

Education and religion both mean a transformation of our inner vision, of our inner hearing, which make for a fundamen-

128

tal attitudinal change. This makes us see the hidden nature of all reality, and gives us an orientation in life. That was our traditional way of including religion and education in a single reality. Now we have a separation between these two, so we speak about religion as something extraneous to education. And we are talking of introducing something called religion *into* education from the outside.

MOHINDER SINGH: I have never studied either religion or education as a discipline. However, I will share a few stray thoughts with you as a student of history. The difficulty with us in India is that we have generally been working with borrowed models. In the field of economics we had earlier borrowed the Marxian model, and created a local brand of the socialist pattern of society. After the decline and fall of the Marxian model, we began to experiment with the capitalist model. My fear is that this model will also fail the way the earlier one failed. We need to evolve a third model, which is based on compassion and justice, and for this I want to take the blessings of His Holiness the Dalai Lama. My friend Dr. Zaidi put forward a very good model; my only worry is that this again is borrowed. Rather than a university in the United States of America, could we not instead turn to the University of Nalanda? But then, the language I am speaking in is a borrowed language, the clothes I wear are a borrowed style. All these have become status symbols that stand in the way of the discovery of our own tradition and heritage.

Regarding education and religion, I cannot say much after a very learned and religious leader of Father Gregorios' standing has spoken. As a student, I remember one line from ancient Indian history: "Vidya Vahin Pashu"—"Without wisdom, without education, one is as an animal." But is 'education' the same as 'wisdom'? Who is educated and who is illiterate? I hold a Ph.D from Delhi University and my grandmother is totally illiterate, but I shall give you one example which will make it very clear that I am more of a *pashu* and she is more of a human being.

My grandmother wanted to visit the Sikh shrine in Himachal Pradesh. Near Ponta Sahib, we had to cross the river Kanua and there was no bridge. We had to sit on a *jhoola* which was then pulled across. The system was that you paid a very small amount for the *jhoola* after crossing the river. But my grandmother insisted on paying in advance. "Suppose I fall in and die, I will die under debt," she said. Now that was education. I am a highly educated, so-called leader. I have taken a loan from the bank to buy a new car. My lawyer advises me that under clause so-and-so I need not pay for three years. So who is educated and who is illiterate? I think my illiterate grandmother had *vidya* and I have but a degree.

As we talk of religion, I am reminded that today happens to be the birthday of Guru Nanak Dev, from whom I have learned a lot. But the problem is that the Nanak of humanity has been reduced by us to being Nanak of Sikhs. My Sindhi brothers are probably the genuine followers of Guru Nanak, because they are not interested in Sikh politics but in the spiritualism of Nanak. But we have brought Sikhism to such a pass that only Mohinder Singh who wears a turban can claim to be a Sikh. This shows how we have reduced religion to formalism.

Thinking about the religious and the secular, it seems that under the influence of western definitions we started believing that one who is religious is necessary communal. I have to quote two examples from history again, of Maulana Azad and Mohammed Ali Jinnah. Azad was a highly religious man and yet he was secular. He did not ask for the partition of India, and did not believe in the two nation theory; he was religious but not communal. Jinnah was secular and also communal.

We are again facing the problem of how to introduce values in education. This creates some difficulties if we introduce these in the way religious education is given in the United Kingdom, for example. They have boys and girls from different religious traditions in a single class. Now, which tradition do they teach, which tradition do they talk about? In a plural secular society this cannot simply be the religion of the majority. Should this then be the 'best' religion and, if so, which is this? Clearly, then, instead of formal religious teachings we need spiritual and moral teachings where the emphasis is on actions rather than rituals. The time has come for us to evolve our own model of religious and modern education.

GEETI SEN: We were talking this morning about the question of education and cultural values, and I was struck by the particular mention of the fact that we have become human resources and not human beings. I have been teaching art history. This subject does not require literacy, an important point in our country. Yet art history can be related to religious values. Art is something we see and imbibe, it stays with us and we gain values from it. It becomes something that does not need to be demonstrated, and it does not need to be dogmatic. It is of concern to me as a teacher to find that there are very, very few schools which will introduce art from the primary level right up to the top class of the school, although I know some have tried to do so.

Art is something which contributes to the psychological and emotional development of the child, inculcating values at a visual level. The values it introduces are pluralistic, and it empowers a multi-disciplinary approach. I was speaking to a dancer who mentioned how she had moved from architecture to dance and had recently begun studying art history, which she found gave her access to religion, philosophy, anthropology, history and sociology. I would like to make an appeal here that it should be introduced in school right from eight years of age upwards.

M.L. SONDHI: Many ideas have been put across in our discussions today, and there has been the suggestion that we could meditate and understand the relevance of these ideas in new situations.

Speaking about India in particular, I think the main problem is one of conflict, violent conflict. Our students in the universities experience this tremendous feeling of the world being at war with itself. It is very relevant that the Nobel Laureate of Peace should be here, bringing us memories of the period when someone from this country went to Tibet and helped the people there to remove negativities and build structures of peace. I refer to Guru Padmasambhava. I would suggest that religious education in a secular society could be looked upon as peace education. Whether it is with the image of Lord Buddha or the image of any of the great religious leaders, The Foundation for Universal Responsibility becomes important as a serious effort to remove deep-rooted conflicts.

Perhaps the beginning of this process is realising that victory is a spurious concept. Europe learned this through the trauma of two World Wars. There is no victory. People just have to come to terms with reality, which is quite different from the ideas they went to war

131

with. We now find that many of the ideas that helped end the Cold War are in fact ideas that His Holiness has spoken about with world leaders. I think his words may have struck some root somewhere. By now it is quite clear that deterrence, security and rigid structures—the games of *realpolitik*—do not make a peaceful world, because *realpolitik* is only the arrangement, analysis and so forth of these spurious concepts. Religious education has to be education for peace, and has to steer clear of the slippery world of *realpolitik*. How do we go about this kind of education? Perhaps music gives us some ideas. Music always deals with sequences and stages, and perhaps we need sequences and stages in the task of conflict resolution. Religion can play a role in the resolution of conflicts. The Vatican has shown this time and again. Lord Buddha himself took various measures towards conflict resolution in various ways. Conflict resolution was attempted by Ramakrishna, and there are many other examples. There is a difference between basic values and instrumental values. In the area of instrumental values, we cannot achieve much; but if we can reach basic values, we can start a new process.

I would like to give an example. I grew up in Punjab, where I was a student of Khalsa college. I am a Hindu, in the tradition of Arya Samaj. During my years at Khalsa College, I learned more about the *Vedas* and about my religion than I would perhaps have learned in any college of my own religion. I remember my teacher, Gurbachan Singh Sahib, who had translated the Guru Granth Sahib into English. I think of him as a kind of catalyst who transformed his students into thinking human beings. He took a class called Religious Instruction, which we all abbreviated to RI, and which with his irrepressible Sikh sense of humour he would call Rigorous Imprisonment. It was possible to laugh together, to appreciate his understanding of the way in which, from Guru Nanak to Guru Gobind Singh, there is a continuous flow of experience of religious ideas, and of spiritual and intellectual achievements. I also learned a great deal about religion, art and architecture from my frequent visits to the Golden Temple and from the poetry which is still part of my life.

None of this was experienced by those students who had studied in DAV colleges or Sanatan Dharam Colleges. The result is that I see the Punjab conflict in entirely different terms from those others. I see it in terms of a culture which has been degraded. The creative urge is there. The aggressive energies can be sublimated and transformed into creative ones. In other words, we have to begin with a universal view of life. We have to work towards the transformation of negativities, as a process of conflict resolution. Every university student should regard himself as a person who is working for peace education. Religion can be interpreted in such a way that we do not move towards an increased use of technology, as the super-powers are doing, but rather towards the inculcating of the creative urge and creative energy.

Religious education in a secular society could in fact be the very basis on which to combine the spiritual values of religion with a modern liberal education. As His Holiness has often said, this cultural evolution can work both ways, much like musical evolution—adaptively or maladaptively. If we could realise that even between a teacher and the taught there is a process of understanding and negotiation, we could also understand that conflict is universal, and we would not be too unhappy when two people fight. As Shakespeare said, "Better is to falling out, all the more endures." We could constructively use some of the building blocks of our experiences. I, for example, am learning from my own experience—as a student in Punjab and as a teacher of Conflict and Peace Studies—to understand how the contradictions involved in striving towards mutually incompatible goals can be overcome.

Maybe we can develop a project which will help us achieve all this. There is for example the Adventures Project in England, which believes that there should be common places of worship. These places provide a space for joint problem-solving, the joint experiencing of situations as well as understanding the relationship between religions. His Holiness has often spoken of a larger, mystical purpose of his coming to India. It is, as it were, that India was to get back from Tibet this kind of mental and spiritual space. Perhaps this is the answer to Tibet's problems also, because it would be absurd for Tibet to be put back into China or be put back anywhere else. In fact, everybody has to loosen up a little bit; there must be more geographical openness, whatever the conflict that is being resolved, be it Punjab or Tibet or Kashmir or Bosnia.

I think the point of this is the attempting to find more such spaces. Perhaps if we cannot find answers right now, then at least we should lie low for a while, and in that abstention we may allow the possibility of map-making for peace. Perhaps this seminar has been an exercise in making a preliminary map of peace and allowing the possibility of new processes to work. It has to be fitted into some mapping of peace, without complaining too much that there is conflict. Because there is bound to be conflict of one type or another. Underlying needs and interests can emerge from religious education in a secular society, so that it does not pose any threat to the future.

S.A. ALI: I think we are giving very different meanings to the two terms 'religion' and 'education'. We all know that the word 'religion' was either derived from the Latin word *religeri*, which means to strive for truth, or *relega* which means unite. To unite man to man and to unite man to God. Unfortunately, religious people today are not striving for the truth, but for a piece of land and worldly possessions. They interpret religion in the second sense, of uniting man to God; in fact, religion today divides people and has lost its meaning.

As far as the second term—education—is concerned, I was told as a child that real education or knowledge is in its totality and not in its fragmented parts. Moreover, it means knowledge about mundane things as well as about metaphysical things and about ultimate reality. But what we receive in schools, colleges and universities today is simply a heap of information. We talk of values but I do not know what others mean by values, because I had a very different set of values when I was a child. Today those values have gone. Unfortunately, our education is becoming shorn of values.

Our Ministry of Human Resources Development acted wisely in forming a committee to explore the introduction of moral education in our curriculum. The committee's report has been accepted by the Government, or so we are told, but we do not know when it is going to be implemented. The problem is that we write reports, we make recommendations, we do all sort of things, but these are either not implemented or, if they are implemented, they take too much time. So our problem is how to get these things implemented efficiently.

RAMACHANDRA GANDHI: My salutations to His Holiness, and thanks to the organisers of this function. Please stop me whenever time requires. I will just tell you a story about something that happened in the modern world, which throws some light on the question of religion. I revisited the University of Oxford about six years ago. An English friend I met asked me if I had seen the Gandhi in the oldest church of the University. I did not know there was a Gandhi in Europe. So I went along with him the following morning and, indeed, I was looking at a mural of Gandhiji on the ceiling. He was sitting cross-legged, wearing John Lennon glasses, looking rather like a gargoyle. Gargoyles are supposed to be carved outside the church to frighten away the evil spirits. Considering what freedom has brought us, we now have to frighten away evil spirits both inside and outside!

I want to offer an interpretation of that gargoyle Gandhi. The mural shows Gandhi with his left arm raised, as if saying that there is truth outside Christianity. With the other hand, he frightens away the evil spirits, the sceptics and cynics, which whisper into our ears that there is no truth inside. Gandhi performs this double service of reminding us that there is truth both within and outside our own religious traditions. I suggest any religious programme in our country might use that emblem on its letter-head. I think it follows from this that there is a sacred duty which every religion in this country must perform. It must openly share with all other traditions, all human beings, without the desire to convert anybody to its religion. I think this is now a matter of responsibility, Your Holiness, for religions to empty themselves of their riches, to offer themselves without condition to everybody. I would regard that as a real act of religious and spiritual education.

This also happens to be in Swami Vivekananda's great Chicago address where, after clearly 100 years of philosophical solitude, the metaphysical and spiritual life of India and Asia was heard in an international tongue at an international forum. Why has no one mentioned God today? Some people do not believe in God, but one who does not believe in God does not believe in himself. I suggest we should not read too much *Vedanta* into this. Communities must let their individuals go their own way, and we must add up all the individual realisations.

SWAMI GOKULANANDA: Your Holiness, distinguished participants...I have been listening to all the previous speakers with rapt attention. One great writer said, and it comes to my mind spontaneously at this moment, that the real prosperity of a nation does not lie in the number of its buildings or material possessions but in its number of real men and women of education, character and integrity. I fully agree with what Ramu Gandhi said just now, that all human beings, and particularly children in their formative stages, have to be taught certain fundamental values of life. Swami Vivekananda once said that the meaning of religion is to be good and to do good to others. I think there is no one even in the 20th century who would take issue with this definition, no one who would not like to be good and to do good to others. But to become good and to do good to others, we have to learn from the deeper religious truths, the fundamental values of life, such as love for truth, for compassion, for selfless service to others, for a sense of oneness and a spirit of dedication. The greater the number of such men and women a country produces, the better for that country and for the entire world.

Father Gregorios made a comment that, as against the western tradition which differentiates between religion and education, our tradition says that both are to be taken together, because both aim at the development and transformation of the inner man. That is why Swami Vivekananda, in two separate definitions of religion and education, makes the same point. He says that education is the manifestation of the perfection already present in man, and religion is the manifestation of his divinity. That means that when we receive religious education in our formative stages, we learn to be conscious of our higher dimension and then we become aware of all kinds of differences and will be able to create a better world.

V.K. MADHAVAN KUTTY: This morning, Father Gregorios asked how a child should be educated. This is an important question. A large number of educational institutions in my State are run by religious institutions, and the authorities are at a loss as to know what to do and how to deal with them. Here's an example: a girl student who stood first in her school was nevertheless denied promotion because she did not belong to the community which is running the school. The current controversy raging in the State is whether children belonging to one religion should be allowed to wear a cap that declares their religious identity. There have been lathi charges over this issue. I come from a State which has attained a 100 percent literacy rate and yet the people at the top level are not really educated. What do we do if the situation continues and this type of virus spreads? Even the educated are becoming victims of undesirable attitudes.

I would like to state one or two instances to demonstrate what education has done to my 'enlightened' State with its 100 percent literacy rate. One of the participants here, Smt. Sugatha Kumari, is running an institution for the poor, the retarded, etc. During a recent visit to the U.S.A. she sought assistance from a Christian organisation which agreed to help her. But the offer was withdrawn the next morning because she was not running the institution exclusively for the Christian community. The next day a Hindu organisation came forward with an offer of help, then they said: "You are doing good work, but there is a photograph of Christ in your office. If you remove this and behave like a true Hindu, we will help you generously." She declined the offer. This is what the present educational system has done to us. How are we to revolt against this? It is not enough to remove State control. It is not enough to hand over control into private hands. What is required is something else.

RAJIV MEHROTRA: The Foundation has been agonising over the issue of what role religious instruction might have in secular societies. We have the situation in the US where the Supreme Court held that prayers should be banned in schools. Given the formal structures of education that are available to us, what mechanism or methodologies can be employed, and what is the moral or secular framework that we might use to transmit and pass on religious values and religious instruction to succeeding generations?

FR. P.M. GREGORIOS: I want to make an off-the-cuff remark in response to Rajiv Mehrotra's question. I think, for example, a form of prayer which is not offensive to any particular religion can be devised by teachers, students, parents and religious leaders consulting with each other. I think this can be worked out in some localities, perhaps not everywhere.

K. VISWANATHAN: I have been working at the grassroots level in a multi-religious community. In Kerala where I live there are Christians, Muslims and Hindus. We do not meet as Christians or Muslims or Hindus but as fellow human beings. We live our lives, we work together, and we also have common prayer, where we allow people to express their own views and let them follow their own vision of truth. A truly religious person will never condemn any other religion. For the last 36 years I have been working at a rural level and so far we have had no problems regarding religion.

We have expressed many ideas at this conference, but I feel that probably there is a gap between action and ideas that needs to be closed. The best way to do this would be for our intellectuals to take part in some active programmes. The second best way would be for intellectuals and workers to come together very often, so that there can be a cross-fertilisation of ideas. I feel, from my own experience, that this is what is lacking. If intellectuals could come together and share their ideas with common people, then we would be able to reach the unreachable and work towards the material, spiritual and cultural development of the people. There are all kinds of factors to consider in such a project. The rural people look towards the city, to the urban elite, what they do, what they say; so there is a great responsibility on the part of the elite also. We have to work at both levels. Along with education of the masses, we should include our own education, to see how we can develop the self-renewal process within ourselves. Often we want to bring about change, without changing ourselves. We are very rigid in our own perceptions. But unless we are willing to undergo a radical transformation in our own ways of thinking and being, we may not be effective instruments in bringing about change in others.

RAGHAV MENON: At the end of the entire day's discussion, I have a sense of despair that nothing practical can be done from discoveries made during the day. The only way we can achieve the issue we have discussed is to subvert the system into decency. There is no other way for radical change, except in the gentle and quiet way change was wrought in traditional India.

NICOLO SELLA: I am coming back to what Rajiv Mehrotra said two minutes ago about religion and education. We have been talking about education as holistic. His Holiness comes from a country where education was, until a few years ago, holistic and he has moved to a country where education is becoming less and less holistic. And he is talking with people from abroad where education has not been holistic for a long time. The impact of the technological and industrial revolution has split education into technology science on one side and moral education on the other. Yet we are making culprits of teachers, or of people linked with education, claiming that they should give us answers which are moral answers. The questions go far deeper and have a longer history than the actions of individual teachers, and so the answers must be sought at deeper levels.

Let us look at schools. Obviously schools have changed today; technology has arrived in them. We have to look at families; what are we doing to help families educate their children? In the West and now increasingly in the East families are becoming smaller and smaller, because grandparents no longer live with the family, and there is a different kind of family set-up. This also has to be taken into account. Then, what can I say about the teaching of religion? In my Catholic country, religious education is decreasing. People are less and less willing to follow religious education. Often this is because the church has difficulties in communicating with the ordinary people.

When we talk about communication, we must also talk about children and young people being exposed to outside communication, through newspapers and journals: what are we doing in these situations? What are we doing to protect and preserve the environment because, again, education is an element of the environment? What we are doing for the self? If we take education as a holistic process, we should look at all these various aspects and try to see what we can do in each.

FR. P.M. GREGORIOS: May I sum up, very briefly, what I heard in this afternoon's discussion? No textbook-bound solution will do. Teaching another subject called religious education will not do. That is clear. Whatever is taught has to be practised first. Religious or moral education cannot be book-based, but has to be relationship-oriented.

139

What are the values to be communicated? Truth is central; it includes integrity, sincerity and an absence of hypocrisy, and it should be taught as a kind of religious ideal. Then there are love, compassion, *karunya*, *ahimsa*; then meditation, prayer, stillness, quietness. I think we have to train people to experience this. Also, the unity of all beings must become the lived experience of children. This is the kind of religious education that we can introduce in schools as well as in other institutions.

KAPILA VATSYAYAN: Your Holiness, you have said that everything is interrelated. Thus the one concern which is being articulated here is that while there might be consciousness of this interconnectedness at the level of intellect and theory, how exactly do we *do* it so that we achieve a greater harmony? This question came up at last year's workshop, and it has come up again. It is all very well to talk in theoretical terms, but now we are on to the important question of action.

H.H. THE DALAI LAMA: I am impressed by the words of various speakers. My special thanks for your different interpretations. According to the conventional understanding, education and religion meant certain things and were defined in a certain way. But that is no more the case. Many issues now seem to fall outside the bounds of what is conventionally understood as religion. Explanations have changed. Medieval philosophy, for instance, held that nothing existed independently, but came into existence due to other factors. Such an interpretation is perfectly acceptable. But that is not of much help in our attempt to understand reality. Diverse interpretations are the business of scholars. Let us leave it to them to discuss.

Our concern is with the problems we are facing and there is hope that we shall solve them. There is a big difference in our thinking today compared to the early years of this century. This change has occurred not because of moral education but because of experience. I think the time has come again to make new adjustments in our thinking because of the experiences we have been through. Through the centuries, many great teachers have taught us to be good human beings but have more or less failed. Today, because of our experience of reality, we are becoming more aware of the need for this. For example, if someone said in the early part of this century that we were responsible for looking after our own people and our planet, nobody would have taken any notice. Now we realise that many injunctions are not just moral statements. Often it is not so much a question of morality as of necessity. We are taking care of the environment today because it is necessary to do so. There is the question of our own survival.

The issue of interdependence is quite a complicated subject, but I usually explain it in this way: I am 57 years old. I have reached the age of 57 not because of my own means and efforts. Over all these years I have needed food and drink. Who provided these? Many people contributed their hard work and finally, in front of me, there is one plate of food. This is a modern city, but you cannot drink water from everywhere. It is only people's hard work that makes drinkable water available. So, obviously, the very survival of this body is due to many other people's efforts, not necessarily intentionally. But nevertheless it happens that way.

I love to see smiling faces. I do not feel happy if I smile and the other person remains serious or unresponding. In order to develop a happier mood, a happier inner feeling, I want someone who responds to me with a smile. I develop friendship, human companionship and compassion with such a person. My happiness cannot develop independently. It depends on other people and even on other forms of life like insects and animals. My happiness is related to the level of family, nation and the whole world. So I may conclude that others' interest is also my interest. That is the reality. When I say 'interdependence' this is what I mean. We cannot neglect the interests of others.

There should be religious and secular ethics; and then we could try to convince everyone that religion is necessary for humanity, but I think this would be difficult. However, we can convince other people that human beings need affection and that without it our future is doomed. As far as religion is concerned, out of five billion people I think there may be around one billion true believers. People may call themselves Christian, Buddhist or Hindu because of their family background, but I do not think they are religious in the real sense of the term. It seems to me the main purpose of religion is transformation, to change oneself. Usually, however, people treat religion as a way of asking for something for themselves. There is no religion without a change in oneself, without self-examination. Our general concept of religion is quite wrong. Something is lacking and this is the necessity to promote the value of human affection.

I am extremely happy to notice quite a number of people who speak with deep feeling, not just artificially. I really feel a sense of commitment, a sense of involvement coming from you. I very much appreciate this. Thank you very much!

PARTICIPANTS AT THE WORKSHOPS

Agrawala SK
Akbar MJ
Ali SA
Anandalakshmy S
Anuradha
Athreya G
Athreya M
Badrinath C
Bhagat U
Bharat Ram M
Bhutalia U
Biswas PG
Bose A
Chabra R
Chandra L
Chaturvedi B
Chaturvedi S
Chaturvedi TN
Chaudhury S
Chauhan VS
Commander A
Dalai Lama HH
Dalal BN
Daswani CJ
Dharmarajan G
Dutta SP
Dutta V
Easley T
Filippi GG
Gandhi R
Ganju MNA

Gokulananda S
Gopinath M
Gregorios PM
Hendrata L
Herzberger R
Hutnik I
Hutnik N
Inamdar S
Inderjit S
Jacob H
Jain GL
Jain LC
Jain M
Jain S
Jaitley J
Jalan K
Jani H
Jani M
John TK
Kakar S
Kapur A
Kapur SS
Kaul H
Khanna K
Khanna M
Kirpal P
Kishwar M
Kumar S
Kumar S
Kumari S
Kutty VKM

Lall JS
Lobzang L
Maira U
Malhotra P
Malik SC
Mansingh S
Martin San A
Mathur B
Mehrotra HN
Mehrotra R
Menon R
Mishra S
Monteluce NS
Mukhopadhyay S
Mulay S
Murthy URA
Nair R
Nair S
Narain S
Ogra A
Pall S
Pande M
Panikulam L
Parikh R
Parthasarathi V
Pema J
Peterson S
Purie R
Rae V
Raina V
Ramdas K

Ramchandani V
Rao MM
Rinpoche A
Rinpoche S
Roy J
Roy P
Roy S
Roy S (B)
Safran YE
Saran M
Sekhar R
Sella N
Sen G
Seth K
Sharma D

Sharma M
Shourie HD
Singh A
Singh M
Singh R
Sinha S
Sivasubramanian V
Sondhi M
Sondhi ML
Talwar GP
Talwar R
Tandon R
Tarter JS
Tiwari V
Tulku D

Vajpeyi A
Vajpeyi K
Vajpeyi R
Vannucci M
Varadarajan M
Varma R
Vasudev A
Vatsyayan K
Verma N
Viswanathan K
Viswanathan VC
Wangyal T
Watanabe E
Zaidi SAR
Zakaria R.